WINNER TAKES ALL

WINNER TAKES ALL

The History of the Championship Play-Off Final

World Football's Richest Game

Aaron Moore

First published by Pitch Publishing, 2025

1

Pitch Publishing
9 Donnington Park,
85 Birdham Road,
Chichester, West Sussex,
PO20 7AJ

www.pitchpublishing.co.uk
info@pitchpublishing.co.uk

A CIP catalogue record is available for this book

from the British Library.

ISBN 978 1 80150 961 9

Typesetting and origination by Pitch Publishing

Printed and bound on FSC® certified paper in line with our continuing commitment to ethical business practices, sustainability and the environment.

Printed and bound by CPI Group (UK) Ltd, Croydon, CR0 4YY

Contents

Introduction 7

The 1990s 27

The 2000s 99

The 2010s 173

The 2020s 233

Introduction

AFTER THE 1986/87 season had drawn to an end, Charlton Athletic were yet to breathe a sigh of relief. The Addicks had finished 19th in the First Division with a final-day victory over Queens Park Rangers, and although they finished ahead of Leicester City, Manchester City and Aston Villa, their threat of relegation to the Second Division wasn't over.

In December 1985, a ten-point plan had been agreed to try and revitalise the financial affairs of the Football League. The plan, known as the Heathrow Agreement, included a restructure of the top division by reducing it from 22 to 20 teams and the introduction of play-offs to facilitate the change. It had been settled that the play-offs would begin in 1987 and last for just two years. A two-legged tie was contested in both the semi-finals and final, with the winner of the play-offs playing in the higher division the following season. For Charlton, this meant facing the three sides that had finished below the automatic promotion places in the Second Division: Oldham Athletic, Leeds United and Ipswich Town.

The change had come at a crucial time for the sport. By the mid-1980s, English football had seen its attendances dwindle. A combination of violence and disaster throughout 1985 forced people away from stadiums across the country and resulted in the Football League needing to make a change. The League Cup semi-final between Chelsea and Sunderland had seen more than 100 people arrested for invasions of the Stamford Bridge pitch; 40 people were injured, of whom 20 were policemen. On 13 March 1985, just nine days after the scenes witnessed at Stamford Bridge, violence flared in an FA Cup match between Luton Town and Millwall. The chaos led to the Hatters banning away supporters after seats were used as missiles against the police.

Disaster then struck in West Yorkshire less than two months later. Bradford City had won the Third Division title, holding a four-point lead over runners-up Millwall and seven points over Hull City. They had had the biggest prize wrapped up in April with a 2-0 win over Bolton Wanderers, and ahead of the final match of the season, against Lincoln City, the crowd had begun their day in a celebratory mood. By the 40th minute, commentator John Helm remarked on a small fire in the main stand. Within four minutes and with windy conditions, the fire had engulfed the whole stand, trapping many in their seats. Some supporters escaped on to the pitch; others weren't so lucky. A total of 56 people died that day and a further 265 were injured.

Three weeks went by before disaster struck again. On 29 May more violence resulted in further lives lost ahead of the European Cup Final between Liverpool and Juventus. Trouble flared for several reasons, but there had been boundless aggression from the Italian fans over the Reds' victory over Roma in the 1984 final. An hour before kick-off saw aggression from both sets of supporters over the flimsy divide between the Liverpool section and what was intended to be a neutral section for those who had bought tickets in Belgium. Objects were thrown between the sets of supporters, but the peak of the aggression came after the throwing of particular items, which included flares, bottles and stones.

The chicken-wire fence was torn down, with Liverpool fans charging at Juventus fans and towards a wall which was the main cause of crushing; 39 people were killed and a further 600 were injured. Those standing closest to the collapsing wall were crushed, and although others escaped by climbing to safety when the wall eventually came down, many others were killed or severely injured. Despite the disaster, the game went ahead to prevent any further trouble, with Juventus winning 1-0. The violence had led to English sides being banned indefinitely from UEFA competitions.

Fans needed to be encouraged to return to stadiums after the 1984/85 season, and to persuade supporters to return, the Football League rejected a £19m television deal before the 1985/86 season to broadcast matches live on the BBC and ITV with league president Jack Dunnett suggesting, 'Football is prepared to have a year or two with no television.'

The 1986/87 play-offs saw Charlton face Ipswich while Oldham went up against Leeds with the first legs of the semi-finals being played on 14 May. Charlton were favourites because of being the highest-ranked side, but their difficult season had made them vulnerable to the teams looking to snatch their place in the top tier.

The only goal at Elland Road had arrived in the 89th minute with Keith Edwards, a substitute who had come on 17 minutes earlier, scoring a near-post header. That had given Leeds the advantage going into the second leg at Boundary Park. That took place three days later and Oldham levelled the tie on aggregate with a goal in the 18th minute after Denis Irwin's cross was diverted into the goal by Gary Williams. A second in the 89th minute had seen another Irwin cross end up in the back of the net, this time headed in by substitute Mike Cecere. The Latics' lead on aggregate only lasted a minute, though, as Edwards drove a ball through a crowd of players to half Oldham's advantage on the night and level the game overall. There weren't any other goals, and extra time wasn't able to separate the sides as Leeds progressed with the away goals rule.

Portman Road had seen the first meeting between Charlton and Ipswich in nearly 20 years, but the first leg didn't see the sides separated. The tenth minute had seen Paul Cooper save a Colin Walsh penalty before Bob Bolder was called into action at the other end when he made a save from Kevin Wilson. Despite Jim Melrose hitting the Ipswich crossbar and Bolder making a double save from efforts by Jason Dozzell and Tony Humes, the game finished goalless. The second leg was held at Selhurst Park, where the Addicks were groundsharing with their south London rivals Crystal Palace. Melrose opened the scoring with a 15-yard header before he doubled the lead with another header two minutes later. Ipswich had looked for a late revival when

Steve McCall tapped home a rebound in the 85th minute, but it had come too late, and Charlton progressed on aggregate.

The final wasn't a goal-fest either. Selhurst Park had seen another late show when Melrose netted in the 87th minute to put the advantage in the hands of the First Division side, but they couldn't make it count in the second leg at Elland Road as Leeds won it 1-0. Brendon Ormsby got the only goal in the 52nd minute and sent the final to a decisive replay at St Andrew's, the home of Birmingham City. In the replay, it took 99 minutes of football before a goal was scored. Leeds' John Sheridan netted from a set piece, but Charlton changed the tide with two quick-fire goals: Peter Shirtliff struck a low shot past Mervyn Day in the 113th minute before he netted a second four minutes later, heading in an Andy Peake free kick. The victory kept the Addicks in the First Division.

The play-offs returned the following season as the Football Association continued to reduce the number of teams in the top tier. Millwall and Aston Villa were promoted to the First Division after finishing first and second in the Second Division respectively, leaving Middlesbrough, Bradford and Blackburn Rovers to fight it out in the play-offs. They had been joined by Chelsea with the Blues finishing 18th in the First Division. Chelsea had only been in the top flight for four seasons following their promotion as Second Division champions in the 1983/84 season but faced relegation if they failed to win the play-offs.

The Blues faced Blackburn in the semi-final and scored the opener a minute into the second half with Gordon Durie curling an effort beyond the Lancashire club's goalkeeper Terry Gennoe. They doubled the lead through Pat Nevin and took a 2-0 lead to Stamford Bridge for the second leg. When it rolled around three days later, it proved a more comfortable affair for the First Division side. A volley from Kevin Wilson had given Chelsea the lead in the 26th minute before Kerry Dixon redirected the ball with his thigh ten minutes into the second half to double their advantage. Scott Sellars pulled one back for Blackburn, but it didn't inspire a late comeback as Chelsea added a further two goals through Wilson and Durie to secure their passage to the final with a 6-1 aggregate win.

Boro had journeyed away for the first leg of the other semi-final, meeting Bradford at Valley Parade on 15 May. It took 67 minutes for the first goal to be scored with Karl Goddard netting for the hosts, but the lead lasted just one minute as Trevor Senior headed Middlesbrough level. Bradford retook the lead almost immediately when Stuart McCall scored from close range. The three goals in three minutes had been enough entertainment for the afternoon as the Bantams took a 2-1 lead into the second leg. The game at Middlesbrough's Ayresome Park wasn't as action-packed with the only goal coming in the 35th minute in favour of the home side, Bernie Slaven scoring. Finishing level on aggregate after two legs, Middlesbrough scored almost immediately into extra time through Gary Hamilton after Bradford defender Lee Sinnott missed a cross and the ball fell to the Boro man. Stephen Pears made two saves from Ian Ormondroyd in the 101st minute and the Teesside club held on.

For the final, Middlesbrough welcomed Chelsea to Ayresome Park in the first leg. It had given them the chance to get off to a good start before they headed to Stamford Bridge in the second leg, and a good start was exactly what they got as a goal from Bernie Slaven gave Boro the lead before Trevor Senior added a second in the final ten minutes of.

The second leg came three days later with Chelsea looking to stay in the top flight. Gordon Durie gave them hope when he opened the scoring in the 18th minute, but it wasn't enough as Middlesbrough won 2-1 on aggregate. The result had relegated Chelsea with Middlesbrough taking their place.

By the end of the 1987/88 season, the play-offs had proved popular among the public, and discussions to have them at the end of each season were taking place. With that decision, the format was altered slightly ahead of 1988/89, with the play-offs being contested by four sides in the same division who had missed out on automatic promotion rather than a team from the league above taking on three other hopefuls looking to seal their place.

The 1988/89 season got under way on 27 August and, while many sides looked for promotion to the top division, it was Chelsea who ran away with the league title. They put the disappointment of the previous seasons behind them, finishing just short of 100 points for the season and holding a 17-point lead over runners-up Manchester City, who had also returned to the First Division. The play-offs were made up of Crystal Palace, Watford, Blackburn and Swindon Town.

The semi-finals came a week or so after the final day of the season. The County Ground saw the only goal come in the 53rd minute when Palace captain Jeff Hopkins scored an own goal after a dangerous cross from Dave Hockaday. After the match, Swindon manager Lou Macari suggested his side were the favourites going into the second leg, despite it being away from home, and he added, 'We shan't be defending.' The sides faced off at Selhurst Park three days later and Crystal Palace took full advantage of being at home. It took just eight minutes for the hosts to take the lead as Mark Bright scored after Paul Digby had beaten away a shot from David Madden. Just before the break, Ian Wright doubled their lead after tucking away his effort from a Bright header and the Eagles progressed 2-1 on aggregate.

Watford's trip to Ewood Park in the first leg was described as hot, hectic, and mostly horrible. The game finished 0-0 with neither side being clinical enough to take an advantage into the second leg. Howard Gayle and Scott Sellars missed chances for the hosts, while Neil Redfearn had the Hornets' best chance of the game, but his effort was saved by Terry Gennoe. The second leg took place three days later at Vicarage Road and Blackburn found themselves ahead when Simon Garner stroked the ball beyond Tony Coton in the Watford goal after taking the ball past a couple of players. Redfearn levelled the tie with a long-range strike in the 29th minute and the game finished 1-1. Extra time followed but there wasn't a change to the scoreline, and Blackburn progressed on the away goals rule.

Blackburn's Ewood Park played host in the first leg on 31 May 1989. The scoring started midway through the first half with Garner flicking a cross from Sellars and Gayle putting the hosts ahead. Just over five minutes later, Gayle netted his second with a half-volley from just outside the box. There weren't many goalscoring opportunities towards the end of the 90, but Palace pulled one back with four minutes left; Eddie McGoldrick scored it. Garner restored the hosts' two-goal cushion in injury time and Rovers took that advantage into the second leg. Once again Crystal Palace made the most of their home advantage and took the lead in the 17th minute as Wright netted from an Alan Pardew cross, before David Madden scored from the penalty spot after Mark Atkins tripped McGoldrick in the box. Palace pulled the game back level in regular time, requiring an extra half an hour to separate the two sides, and the difference came in the 117th minute with Wright netting his second of the afternoon after he latched on to a cross from McGoldrick. The 4-3 win on aggregate saw Crystal Palace promoted to the First Division.

The play-offs had seen two changes ahead of the 1989/90 season with the final being contested in a one-off game at Wembley rather than as a two-legged affair.

Swindon Town faced Sunderland in the first final at Wembley, with Alan McLoughlin scoring the only goal to seal his team's promotion to the top flight. Or so they thought. Events behind the scenes with their owner meant the Robins' success became null and void, with Sunderland promoted in their place.

The 1990 crowd of almost 73,000 was down by over 12,000 a year later when Brighton & Hove

Albion faced Notts County, but the game didn't disappoint for County fans. The Magpies had faced Middlesbrough in the semi-finals, travelling to Ayresome Park for the first leg and opening the scoring through Phil Turner when he chipped Dave Regis's pass over Andy Dibble in the Middlesbrough goal. Boro got back on terms through Jimmy Phillips, who turned in a John Hendrie cross, with the match ending level. The second leg was three days later, and after a goalless first half, Paul Harding scored his first professional goal to put County ahead in the 78th minute with a header. That was enough to send Neil Warnock's team through as they won 2-1 on aggregate.

Brighton had just qualified for the play-offs, with a free kick in the last minute of the final game of the season against Ipswich Town to seal a 2-1 win, which carried them into sixth place, despite having a negative goal difference. Their first leg against Millwall saw them concede after 14 minutes: a poor clearance from Ştefan Iovan found Paul Stephenson whose shot from 25 yards beat Perry Digweed in the Brighton goal. In the 40th minute, the Seagulls were level as Mark Barham took advantage of poor defending from David Thompson, then another defensive error saw Mike Small intercept a weak back pass in the 53rd minute to put Brighton ahead. The scoring didn't stop there: three minutes later, Clive Walker added a third and, in the 60th minute, Robert Codner scored from a Small pass to make it 4-1. The return leg followed three days later with Millwall's John McGlashan scoring early in the first half, but again Brighton turned it around. A minute after the break, Codner levelled the match when he converted a cross from Small, before John Robinson scored his first goal for the Seagulls to make it 2-1, sealing a 6-2 win over the London side.

In the final, Brighton started on the offensive, but it was County who took the lead. A controversial corner in the 29th minute after the ball appeared to have gone out off a Notts County player was played short to Turner whose cross was met by Johnson to finish past Digweed. County got their second in the 59th minute when Johnson beat Digweed from a narrow angle, and 13 minutes later Regis scored to make it 3-0. Colin Pates had headed out a Draper free kick but it struck Regis who bundled the ball over the line. Dean Wilkins scored a late consolation goal after John Byrne sent in a low cross but the 3-1 win for County saw them promoted to the top flight for the first time in seven years.

Before the formation of the Premier League, the last promotion to the then top-tier First Division was fought for between Blackburn Rovers and Leicester City. It would mark the start of Leicester's three consecutive play-off finals, losing to Blackburn in 1992 and Swindon in 1993 before finally going up against Derby County in 1994; the Lancashire club sealed promotion with a penalty scored by Mike Newell in the 45th minute.

Winner Takes All details the highs, lows and riches that come with the Championship play-off final, starting from the 1992/93 season following the creation of the Premier League.

The 1990s

1992/93

First Division play-off final

31 May 1993

Leicester City 3 (Joachim 57; Walsh 68; Thompson 69)

Swindon Town 4 (Hoddle 42; Maskell 47; Taylor 53; Bodin 84 pen)

FOLLOWING THEIR semi-final disappointment in 1988/89, Swindon Town were condemned to the Second Division once again but, despite a turbulent season, they found themselves in the play-offs alongside Newcastle United, Blackburn Rovers and Sunderland in the spring of 1990. Their first win of the season hadn't come until 26 September when the Robins defeated Plymouth Argyle, but it was a win enough to spark a little bit of form: further wins over Hull City, Ipswich Town, Oxford United, Brighton, Stoke City and Middlesbrough and a draw against Bradford City saw Swindon lose just once in a run of nine games before they faced a 2-0 defeat to Port Vale.

Mid-December to mid-March had seen Swindon win nine, draw three and lose one, boosting their position in the table. That impressive run had been ended by a defeat to Hull with the loss to the Tigers knocking Swindon slightly off-course. Back-to-back defeats were followed by just two points over the next two matches before a win on the road against AFC Bournemouth had looked to be the springboard to another good run of form, but it wasn't. The Robins beat Watford and West Bromwich Albion at home but only managed to pick up nine points in seven games: losses to Brighton & Hove Albion and Blackburn with the other three points coming in three consecutive draws in the final three matches of the regular season, against Newcastle, Middlesbrough, and Stoke City. The final league positions meant the play-offs would see a north-east derby between Newcastle and Sunderland in one semi-final and a matchup between Blackburn and Swindon in the other.

Swindon's first leg was played on 13 May at Ewood Park. The table had suggested a dogfight between the three sides below Newcastle, with only goal difference separating them. Swindon knew they needed to make the most of finishing fourth, but the play-offs were a completely different prospect.

A goal from Steve White had given the visitors the lead after 30 minutes. Swindon continued to dominate, and their advantage was doubled in the second half with Peter Foley's volley from 25 yards in the 55th minute. Blackburn managed to get themselves on the scoresheet as Andy Kennedy scored on 73 minutes, but it didn't spark a comeback and Swindon led going into the second leg three days later. The Robins used being at home to their advantage and extended their aggregate lead. A weak back pass from Rovers defender David Mail allowed Duncan Shearer to intercept and score before he doubled their lead on the day minutes later. He charged down the left and saw his pass converted by White from close range. Again, Blackburn pulled one back with a goal midway through the second half as Howard Gayle's 30-yard strike was deflected by Ross MacLaren past Fraser Digby. That only proved to be another consolation as Swindon progressed to the final.

The north-east derby didn't prove fruitful; the first leg at Roker Park in Sunderland had been ill-tempered but produced nothing in the way of shots on target, meaning it finished goalless. However, the tie at St James' Park was different. Eric Gates opened the scoring when he converted a low cross from Gary Owers to give the visitors the lead before the only other goal of the game came in the 86th minute. Again, it went the way of the visitors, to the despair of the home fans who invaded the pitch, with Marco Gabbiadini netting. With the second leg finishing 2-0, it was Sunderland fans who were making their way to Wembley for the play-off final.

While the football had been played on the pitch, behind the scenes Swindon Town's owner Brian Hillier was under investigation. He had been arrested in January 1990 under suspicion of defrauding the Inland Revenue as well as placing bets against his own team losing in the 1987/88 FA Cup but, despite these allegations, the Robins continued in their quest for promotion to the First Division.

Over 70,000 supporters made their way to London on 28 May 1990 to see Swindon face Sunderland, and whether people expected either of these sides to be at Wembley for the play-off final was up for debate, but nobody cared about that. The Black Cats made a better start to the game but Swindon were the more dominant team, and missed a few good chances before they took the lead midway through the first half when Alan McLoughlin scored from a deflected effort off Gary Bennett from just outside the box, a large deflection taking the ball beyond Tony Norman in the Sunderland goal. Swindon had further chances to extend their lead in the second half, but they couldn't take them, and the game finished 1-0. The result saw them promoted to the First Division for the first time in their history and earned them their third promotion in five seasons to join the top flight.

The celebrations didn't last long as Brian Hillier appeared in court shortly after their triumph at Wembley. Having been up for 36 charges for financial irregularities, he was found guilty and, as a result, Swindon were demoted two divisions. That had taken them from the First Division to the Third Division, but on appeal it had been reduced to one division and they returned to the second tier ahead of the 1990/91 season. In their place, Sunderland were promoted to the top flight, although Newcastle had argued it should have been them, with the Geordies finishing third and higher than the two sides who had competed in the play-off final.

The following season hadn't been a repeat of the previous as Swindon had felt a hangover effect and it had become apparent they were facing a relegation battle rather than competing for promotion again. Their form remained inconsistent throughout the season, but the Robins managed to narrowly avoid relegation at the end of 1990/91 with 50 points, ahead of Hull and West Brom, who both went down, with only two teams being relegated that year. Swindon manager Ossie Ardiles had resigned to take charge of Newcastle United, so the club had turned to Tottenham legend Glenn Hoddle, who took over in April 1991. Hoddle guided the Robins to safety before his first full season in charge saw a change in the Wiltshire side's fortunes. A record of 18 wins, 15 draws and 13 losses saw them finish five points off the play-offs, but it was something to build upon.

Before the start of the 1992/93 season got under way, the Football League had undergone a huge reshuffle. A decision by First Division clubs had been taken on 20 February 1992 to form a new league, known as the FA Premier League. The idea behind it was to prevent the top clubs from losing income to lower divisions and to maximise their bargaining position ahead of the renewal of new television deals. It meant more revenue, improved club autonomy and increased global appeal, creating a more competitive top tier. The reshuffle meant the Second Division had become the First Division and the Third and Fourth Divisions had become the Second and Third, respectively.

The creation of the Premier League had given the opportunity for a TV deal which, at the time, was the biggest in the history of British sport. The inaugural deal had been signed in May 1992 and, under it, Sky paid £304m for the first five seasons of the league, covering 1992/93 to 1996/97. Clubs were competing for more than the standard prize money given at the end of the season based on each individual position in the table. Now they had

TV money that would boost the coffers, and this sort of finance was essential to thriving in a competitive market.

In the newly named First Division, Swindon finished fifth in 1992/93. The Robins won 21 of their 46 games while drawing 13 and losing 12. Their final league position saw them join Portsmouth, Tranmere Rovers and Leicester City in the play-offs for a place in the Premier League.

The Robins faced Tranmere in the play-off semi-final while Leicester went up against Portsmouth. The first leg for Swindon saw them welcome Tranmere to the County Ground and within two minutes Nicky Summerbee's cross had been headed into his own goal by Steve Vickers. The good start continued a minute later as Hoddle's team found themselves 2-0 ahead when Dave Mitchell made the most of a mishandled shot. A goal from Tranmere in the fourth minute was disallowed for a push on Hoddle, but they did find themselves back in the game in the 27th minute as John Morrissey was on target for the visitors. It hadn't been enough for a fightback as Swindon added a third in the second half with Craig Maskell scoring. The second leg at Prenton Park also saw Swindon take the lead, this time on the half-hour mark; Martin Ling played a ball through to John Moncur, who dispatched his shot well. The game was level just before half-time as Mark Proctor scored a volley before Pat Nevin added a second for the hosts after Fraser Digby dropped a cross. Maskell equalised, making it 5-3 on aggregate, but Tranmere added a third of the evening with Kenny Irons scoring from the penalty spot. Although they lost the second leg 3-2, the Robins had edged the tie on aggregate and progressed to the final.

Leicester's Filbert Street ground was under redevelopment so the first leg of their semi-final with Portsmouth was played at Nottingham Forest's City Ground, but it hadn't been an exciting affair and was described as dreadful by Paul Weaver in *The Guardian*. The only thing saving the day was a stunning strike from Julian Joachim, with the game finishing 1-0. The second leg was three days later, and the first half remained largely uneventful. Portsmouth levelled the tie on aggregate six minutes into the second half as Alan McLoughlin scored from a George Lawrence header but Leicester immediately responded to put the score back into their favour with a goal two minutes later when Ian Ormondroyd found the target after getting on to the end of a deflected effort. The 69th minute saw Leicester take the lead on the night through Steve Thompson with a shot from the edge of the box but, again, it was extinguished fast. Bjørn Kristensen curled an effort into the far corner from 18 yards for Pompey but the draw wasn't good enough and Leicester progressed on aggregate.

The final was right at the end of May, and it didn't disappoint. Leicester had hoped to change their fortunes in their second final in as many years while Swindon sought promotion to the top division after missing out in 1990. Swindon raced into a 3-0 lead with Glenn Hoddle, Craig Maskell and Shaun Taylor scoring. Leicester had looked dead and buried, but they had other ideas as Julian Joachim pulled one back before a quick-fire double from Steve Walsh and Steve Thompson brought them level. With the Robins pushing to put themselves back ahead, they had the chance to do so in the 84th minute when Steve White went down in the box. Paul Bodin stepped up and tucked the ball beyond Kevin Poole in the Leicester goal. That proved to be the winner as Town were promoted to the Premier League for the first time in their history.

After securing promotion, player-manager Glenn Hoddle left to take charge of Chelsea with his assistant, John Gorman, accepting the club's offer to become the new manager. The Robins had seen Colin Calderwood move to Tottenham for £1.35m and looked to strengthen the team with the signings of Luc Nijholt, Adrian Whitbread and Jan Åge Fjørtoft for a combined total of £1.175m. The following season didn't see Swindon win until late November with a victory at home to Queens Park Rangers. That was the first of only five wins throughout the entire season with the Robins picking up another 15 points from draws, but it wasn't enough to keep them in the top flight. With 30 points, and having conceded 100 goals, Swindon were relegated back to the First Division and haven't returned since.

* * *

Martin Ling had played in all but two games for Swindon during the 1992/93 season so I spoke to him about the club's promotion to the Premier League.

You joined Swindon Town in March 1991, two years after their disappointment of not being admitted to the top flight. When you joined was there still a consensus to achieve promotion?

ML: The players that were there still had a bugbear about it. There wasn't masses of players still there from that season, but the ones who remained continued to talk about the injustice. As players you are always going to feel that you've done the job in the playing sense, but then to have it taken away, that feeling is always going to be there.

After finishing 21st in the 1990/91 season, the club massively improved and finished eighth in the Second Division. What changed to achieve a huge jump?

ML: Glenn Hoddle coming in was the biggest change. The emphasis on playing good football was within most of the players already. He kept the club out of the relegation zone and then implemented ideas that he had picked up from Monaco. The new enlightenment was brought to the new players and it just clicked. We were always in the top half and always had an outside chance of the play-offs, before we carried that into the following season.

When the Premier League was created, what were your thoughts on it and the money that was involved?

ML: The English football pyramid had always been the same, just with the leagues under different names, but the introduction of the Premier League and the teams that were involved had made it a more lucrative league to get amongst. It was talked about, but there was a lot of apprehension around what it meant. I think a lot of supporters thought it was just the so-called big boys trying to pull away, but for the players it was just about being in the top league, regardless of what it was called.

You secured a play-off spot with a fifth-placed finish and faced Tranmere Rovers in the semi-final. Was a play-off spot the target for the season or was it a surprise to find yourselves among the top six?

ML: After we had finished eighth the previous season, we believed if we could add players to the squad we already had, we would stand a chance. We always felt we had the edge over Tranmere Rovers, especially with the lead from the first leg. Once we got ahead, we kept our noses in front, but they were always on our tail. As a footballer, you must keep your mind on the task at hand and you can understand why they say it is a nervy affair.

Leicester had lost the previous play-off final. Did that change your mindset going into the

1993 final, knowing they had the experience of the previous one?

ML: We certainly went into that game as underdogs. Leicester were considered one of the big teams, not quite as big as they have been, but they were certainly up there when we played them. I was one of the players going to Wembley for the first time, but we still had our own experience within the squad of playing there. One of the things that helped was visiting Wembley the day before the final.

The final you were involved in is considered one of the best because of the scoreline. After going 3-0 ahead and being pegged back to 3-3, did you feel you had lost your chance at promotion?

ML: When we got our third just after half-time, a lot of us felt we had done what we needed to. You keep the concentration up because we know you need to keep yourself ahead, but they just took their shackles off at 3-0 and for 15 minutes they just bombarded us. There was still a belief, despite it feeling like everything was falling around us, that we still have a chance, and it wasn't like it went level and we were clinging on. We took control of the game again and had to eliminate the thoughts that we might have blown our chance at promotion.

A penalty in the 84th minute secured the victory. What were your feelings when that penalty was scored and after promotion had been confirmed?

ML: Whether it was a penalty or not has been argued for a long time. Steve White says he was touched and fell to the floor. We all believed it was a penalty, but it's one of those that is sometimes given and sometimes not given. It was the most important penalty Paul Bodin had scored, and I was sure to let him know in the celebration.

Swindon's first season in the Premier League ended in relegation. What were factors that led to the immediate return to the First Division?

ML: We lost three of our big components. Glenn [Hoddle] going to Chelsea was a big miss as a manager and secondly as a player. Then we lost Colin Calderwood who was our captain, and a lad called Dave Mitchell, who was probably one of the most underrated players at the club. Before you lose those three, you go into the season thinking everything will be all right and we'll be fine. We made some good signings, but it was more difficult than anyone had given it credit for. We had found our feet in the second half of the season, but the start didn't give us any leeway.

* * *

Season 1993/94

First Division play-off final

30 May 1994

Derby County 1 (Johnson 28)

Leicester City 2 (Walsh 41, 84)

Leicester City had missed out on promotion to the Premier League with a loss to Swindon Town in the 1992/93 play-off final, but they bounced back to find themselves in the final once again – their third appearance in the showcase game in as many years having also lost to Blackburn Rovers in 1991/92.

The Foxes had narrowly avoided relegation at the end of the 1990/91 season; their two-point lead over West Bromwich Albion had given them the opportunity to improve their fate and that's exactly what they did. After spells with Wolverhampton Wanderers and Darlington, Brian Little was brought in as manager and immediately turned Leicester into play-off contenders. Under his management, the 1991/92 season had seen Leicester finish fourth after a good start, which set them up for the next nine months, taking 13 points from their opening five games. A third of their losses had come by mid-October, and they went on to win 77 points from their 46 games, which was more than enough to see them reach the play-offs, alongside Derby County, Cambridge United and Blackburn.

Leicester met Cambridge in the semi-finals and there was little to separate the two sides in the first leg, which finished level after Kevin Russell's volley just before half-time was cancelled out by Daniel O'Shea's header in the 76th minute. When the sides met three days later, Leicester were far more clinical and showed their class. Filbert Street came alive with a five-star performance from the Foxes, who won 5-0, seeing them progress 6-1 on aggregate. Tommy Wright had made the most of a Richard Wilkins defensive miskick and Steve Thompson made it 2-0 seven minutes later. Three goals followed in five second-half minutes to seal a comfortable victory for Leicester: Russell headed home in the 59th minute before Wright scored from an Ian Ormondroyd pass and the latter netted a fifth.

Blackburn had also made the most of their home advantage as they sealed a 4-2 win over Derby County in the first leg. The Rams had raced into a 2-0 lead in the first quarter of an hour with Marco Gabbiadini heading in the opener from a Paul Simpson free kick and Tommy Johnson scored having been put through by Simpson with a chip, but by half-time the scores were level. Scott Sellars halved the deficit with a free kick which took a significant deflection before Mike Newell scored their second. Midway through the second half, David Speedie put the home side ahead after capitalising on a defensive mistake from Andy Comyn before adding his second of the match a minute later. Derby had looked to fight back in the second leg at the Baseball Ground with goals from Comyn and Ted McMinn, but their 2-1 win after Kevin Moran had initially equalised for Blackburn wasn't enough and Rovers qualified for the final.

The final was far from a goal-fest that some may have expected, and the only score came in the final minute of the first half. A long ball from Colin Hendry was headed back by Newell to Speedie with the latter being brought down in the box by Steve Walsh. Newell stepped up and struck the ball into the bottom corner past Carl Muggleton. That was enough for Blackburn to reach the Premier League, but the goal remained controversial after the game had ended. Walsh had accused Speedie of diving, saying he had done what all strikers would do to win a penalty, but the only thing that mattered to Blackburn was their promotion.

Leicester had almost had a replica run in 1992/93, picking up one fewer point than they did during the previous season, and it was enough to qualify for the play-offs for the second consecutive year. The Foxes had hoped to use the disappointment of a year earlier but again they fell short, losing 4-3 in the final to Swindon Town. The conversation turned to whether Leicester would eventually reach the top flight, and the 1993/94 season offered that opportunity.

It wouldn't be Leicester's best of their three play-off seasons, but the Foxes still finished fourth with another haul of over 70 points. They didn't have any awful runs of form; the worst they recorded was a three-game losing streak, but unbeaten runs that had far more draws than wins had certainly prevented them finishing higher. With that, they were ten points off Nottingham Forest in the automatic promotion spots and a point behind third-placed Millwall.

The semi-finals had paired Leicester with Tranmere, and Millwall against Derby. The first leg at Tranmere's Prenton Park had finished goalless with one of the best chances falling to the home side, but John Aldridge's close-range shot was saved by the fingertips of Foxes keeper Gavin Ward. The return leg came three days later at Filbert Street. The opening goal had come in the final moments of the first half when Mark Blake's shot off the post was tapped in by Ian Ormondroyd, but the game was levelled again on the other side of half-time when Pat Nevin converted a Ged Brannan cross. David Speedie, who had come on as a substitute, restored Leicester's lead with four minutes remaining with a header. The match had ended 2-1 to Leicester, putting them through to the final, but it wasn't without incident: both Speedie and Tranmere keeper Eric Nixon were sent off for getting into an altercation with only seconds remaining.

Millwall travelled to the Baseball Ground on 15 May, but it was the hosts who opened the scoring when midway through the first half Gordon Cowans fired a low effort past Kasey Keller after the goalkeeper failed to gather Paul Simpson's effort off the post. Derby held the foothold in the game, and it showed when they doubled their lead on the hour as Tommy Johnson scored after being sent clear by Gabbiadini. The New Den hosted the second leg three days later but it was marred by two pitch invasions by the home supporters. The Rams' aggregate lead was increased when Gabbiadini converted Mark Pembridge's cross after 16 minutes, and Millwall's uphill battle became steeper when Johnson doubled the score on the night six minutes later. Pat Van Den Hauwe's own goal extended Derby's advantage before Greg Berry reduced the deficit in the 60th minute but it wasn't enough, and the Rams progressed 5-1 on aggregate.

The final took place on 30 May with Derby taking the lead in the 28th minute after teasing some early shots. Simpson's through ball found Johnson who outran both Simon Grayson and Brian Carey before scoring past Ward, but just before half-time Leicester were level. Iwan Roberts had blocked Martin Taylor in the Derby goal as the shot-stopper tried to reach Gary Coatsworth's cross, but with referee Roger Milford failing to penalise the foul, Walsh headed the loose ball goal-bound. Paul Williams failed to clear his lines and the score was level, as it remained until the 84th minute. After Leicester had come close just two minutes earlier, Grayson made a run down the right-hand side and his pass was met by the head of Ormondroyd. Taylor made the save, but the ball fell to Walsh who scored his second of the game and sealed a 2-1 victory for the Foxes.

Leicester were tipped for relegation before the 1994/95 Premier League season had begun. Their seven-year exile from the top flight and a couple of failed attempts at promotion during the previous campaigns was not enough to convince anyone that the outcome would be different. Their season had begun with just two wins in the opening ten games and that had given supporters an idea of how they'd fare throughout the next few months. Leicester won just four more games and picked up a further 11 points through draws but that wasn't enough to paper over the 25 losses they incurred in their 42 matches. The Foxes had also lost their manager, Brian Little, in November 1994. He had been linked with Aston Villa but with the West Midlands side not appointing a successor to Ron Atkinson,

Little resigned as manager. Within days of departing Filbert Street, he was appointed the manager at Villa Park. His replacement, Mark McGhee, was unable to prove the critics wrong and Leicester were relegated alongside Crystal Palace, Ipswich Town and Norwich City.

* * *

Season 1994/95

First Division play-off final

29 May 1995

Bolton Wanderers 4 (Coyle 75; De Freitas 86, 118; Paatelainen 105)

Reading 3 (Nogan 4; Williams 12; Quinn 119)

(After extra time)

Bolton Wanderers had been promoted from the third tier at the end of the 1992/93 season to the newly rebranded First Division after finishing second behind Stoke City by three points. They had enjoyed a good campaign, winning just over half of their games, but it wasn't without its poor runs of form. After drawing 0-0 with Stoke on 5 September, Bolton only took an additional two points in a run of eight games before facing a run of just two points in four fixtures at the end of January.

Their return to the First Division had seen them finish a respectable 14th in 1993/94. Their bottom-half placing had been mainly down to their start to the season; two points from the opening three games hadn't been the best start to life back in the second tier and by 6 November Bolton had won just four times. They found some form after that, losing just twice between early November and early February, but again lost form, with a lone win over Charlton Athletic being their only one in a run of 11 games.

Bolton arguably had a worse start to the 1994/95 season with a single point in the opening three games. Their form hadn't been great before the beginning of October, but they soon found some results and between October and the end of 1994 they lost just three times. That was in a run of 17 games and was followed by another run of one defeat in 15, putting the Wanderers in a strong position towards the end of the season. The remaining six matches of the season saw them win one, draw two and lose three but, despite their poor form at the end, Bolton finished third and alongside Reading, Wolverhampton Wanderers and Tranmere Rovers in the play-offs.

The play-off semi-finals had pitted both Wanderers together with Bolton travelling to Wolverhampton on 14 May. Steve Bull opened the scoring just before half-time with a header from a Robbie Dennison cross, but the equaliser for Bolton came early in the second half when Jason McAteer scored with a chip, before Don Goodman's header across the face of goal was headed in by Mark Venus to restore Wolves' lead. The second leg took place three days later and Bolton had the lead in the 44th minute with a goal from John McGinlay to level the tie at 2-2. That was the only goal of the game, with extra time needed to decide the winners, and McGinlay's second with 11 minutes remaining was the clincher as Bolton progressed to the final.

Reading travelled to Tranmere's Prenton Park for their opening leg, and it didn't take long for the visitors to go in front with Stuart Lovell striking a volley from Lee Nogan's cross. Tranmere struck back seven minutes later through Chris Malkin, who headed in a cross from John Morrissey. Reading retook the lead in the 75th minute through Nogan before Lovell made it 3-1 after scoring from a rebounded Nogan effort. There was no change to the aggregate score as the second leg finished goalless, putting Reading into the final.

At Wembley, Reading came out of the blocks the quickest, and took the lead after just four minutes when Nogan received the ball from Andy Bernal, beat two players and shot past goalkeeper Keith Branagan. The lead was doubled in the 12th minute as Simon Osborn's quickly taken free kick was met by the well-timed run of Ady Williams, who also steered it beyond Branagan, and Reading went into the break with a 2-0 lead. It took until the 75th minute for Bolton to pull one back as McGinlay's cross found Owen Coyle at the far post and, by outjumping his opponent, the forward was able to head it beyond Shaka Hislop. A further ten or so minutes later, Fabian de Freitas equalised for Bolton after latching on to a through ball from Alan Thompson and striking it low past Hislop.

There were no further goals so extra time was needed to settle the final.

Right at the end of the first period of extra time, Bolton had the lead for the first time in the match with a header from Paatelainen. It was almost déjà vu in the second period as Bolton added a fourth with two minutes remaining, De Freitas converting the rebound after his initial effort hit the post. Reading had an extremely small glimmer of hope right at the end of extra time as player-manager Jimmy Quinn scored a minute later, but it had come too late, and Bolton were 4-3 winners.

After a 15-year exile from the top flight, Bolton's first season in the Premier League had gone terribly. With Jason McAteer, Owen Coyle and Mark Seagraves departing the club in the summer for around £5.8m, they had to bring in reinforcements: Gerry Taggart, Saša Ćurčić and Steve McAnespie were signed for around £4.9m. The Wanderers won just ten points by the new year, leaving them bottom of the table, and with that came more investment in a bid to save themselves from relegation. The Greater Manchester side spent more than £3m with the additions of Nathan Blake from Sheffield United for £1.68m as well as Scott Sellars, Gavin Ward, Scott Taylor and Wayne Burnett for a combined £1.49m.

Their start to the season had seen manager Roy McFarland sacked on New Year's Day with his assistant, Colin Todd, taking over. In the second half of the season Bolton's form improved, and after winning just two games before the turn of the year they won six in 1996 and drew against Manchester City, but 19 points wasn't enough as they finished 20th and were relegated straight back to the second tier.

* * *

Season 1995/96

First Division play-off final

27 May 1996

Crystal Palace 1 (Roberts 14)

Leicester City 2 (Parker 76 pen; Claridge 120)

(After extra time)

Following their immediate relegation from the Premier League, Leicester sought to bounce back again in 1995/96. The financial impact of relegation had been reduced with the sale of Mark Draper to Aston Villa for £3.25m. His sale had come just a season after Leicester had paid a club-record fee to Notts County for the player, securing his services for £1.25m, but the cash windfall certainly helped.

After a mixed start to the season, Leicester had only lost three games by the end of October. Two wins to begin November wasn't enough to embark on a lengthy run of form as the Foxes won just twice between mid-November and March, taking an additional nine points from draws. During the season, Mark McGhee left unexpectedly to join Wolverhampton Wanderers and was replaced by Martin O'Neill. Four wins and four losses had been followed by a five-game unbeaten run in which they took 13 points from a possible 15. Despite their drops in form, Leicester finished in fifth, qualifying for the play-offs.

They faced Stoke City on 12 May and secured a goalless first leg, with the only real highlight coming in the fifth minute when Kevin Poole made a save from Graham Potter. *The Guardian*'s Michael Walker compared the save to Gordon Banks's 'save of the century' against Pelé in the 1970 World Cup. The second leg followed three days later at the Victoria Ground and the first half remained goalless, but Garry Parker had Leicester ahead within

30 seconds of the start of the second half. The goalscorer had only just been restored into the team after a disagreement with O'Neill, but his volley from a Scott Taylor cross was important as the Foxes progressed to the final with a 1-0 aggregate win.

In the other semi-final, Charlton Athletic welcomed south London rivals Crystal Palace to The Valley. The hosts made the most of their home advantage with a goal in the first minute as Shaun Newton capitalised on a rebound from Palace keeper Nigel Martyn. In the 65th minute, Kenny Brown equalised with a volley, but Crystal Palace regained the lead six minutes later: Carl Veart's header from a George Ndah overhead kick made it 2-1. The return leg at Selhurst Park saw the only goal come in the third minute when Ray Houghton floated an effort into the top corner. Charlton's David Whyte had had a second-half goal disallowed after he was adjudged to be offside and the game finished 1-0, sending Crystal Palace to the final with a 3-1 aggregate victory.

Leicester had been dominant in the early stages at Wembley, but it was Palace who took the lead when Andy Roberts struck an effort from the edge of the box, beating Kevin Poole in the Leicester goal. The lead lasted until the 76th minute when Leicester were awarded a penalty after Steve Walsh had passed to Muzzy Izzet, who was brought down in the box by Marc Edworthy. Martyn had managed to get a hand to Parker's spot kick, but it wasn't enough to stop the ball going in. There was nothing to separate the two sides and the game went to extra time, which very nearly wasn't enough to find a winner. Leicester had made a change in the last minute in preparation for penalties as goalkeeper Zeljko Kalac was brought on. The 6ft 7in Australian wasn't needed, though, as Steve Claridge struck the winner from a Julian Watts header to secure Leicester's return to the top flight.

Before 1996/97 began, Leicester were once again tipped for an immediate return to the First Division. Martin O'Neill's task for the season was to achieve survival and prove the critics wrong. The Foxes had strengthened their squad to achieve this with the signings of Spencer Prior (£600,000 from Norwich City), Kasey Keller (£900,000 from Millwall) and Ian Marshall (£800,000 from Ipswich Town), and a ninth-placed finish was what they got. Leicester spent six seasons in the Premier League, achieving a top-ten finish in four of them before they were relegated at the end of the 2001/02 season when finishing bottom.

* * *

Season 1996/97

First Division play-off final

26 May 1997

Crystal Palace 1 (Hopkin 90)
Sheffield United 0

Alan Smith had been sacked within days of relegation from the Premier League at the end of the 1994/95 season with Steve Coppell returning to the position after almost two years away, having previously left in May 1993.

The campaign had only seen Palace sit in the relegation zone towards the start and end, while bouncing around mid-table in between. A poor start with four points in seven games had been followed by a mixed run of results that had left the south Londoners dwindling away from danger but adrift of the top end. Despite a run of four points in nine games between November and the new year, Palace hadn't dropped back into the relegation zone until a goalless draw with Aston Villa at Selhurst Park on 4 April, and from there they couldn't escape.

Relegation had also resulted in an exodus of players to other teams. Chris Armstrong went to Tottenham for £6m, Chris Coleman moved to Blackburn for £4.9m and Gareth Southgate remained in the top flight with Aston Villa for a fee of around £3.75m. Other departures had included Richard Shaw, Ricky Newman, Iain Dowie, Darren Patterson and Andy Preece, who all went for fees between £250,000 and £1.5m. Palace's team was unrecognisable for the 1995/96 season, but they still hoped for a return to the Premier League.

They almost did it at the first time of asking. After winning just four times between August and the start of December, Crystal Palace went on a run that saw them lose just once in 21 games. That run had stretched from early December to early April before a defeat to Leicester City had ended it. The final five matches of the season had seen them win three consecutive games before losing their last two, but they did finish third and qualify for the play-offs, despite losing some of their big-name players at the start of the season.

They fell short of promotion under the management of Dave Bassett, who had taken over from Coppell in February. The latter had spent seven months back at the club, but with relegation looking increasingly likely, he departed. Under Bassett, Palace's fortunes changed, and they comfortably marched into the play-offs where, after defeating Charlton 3-1 on aggregate in the semi-final, their hearts were broken by a late Steve Claridge goal against Leicester at Wembley.

Bassett continued as manager into the 1996/97 season but only remained at the club until late February, leaving to join Premier League strugglers Nottingham Forest, so Steve Coppell returned to the manager's chair. Bassett had won 13, drawn ten and lost nine of the games he was in charge of before Coppell saw out the last 15 games with a record of won six, drew four and lost five. It hadn't been a bad season, though, and Crystal Palace found themselves in the play-offs once again.

The Eagles faced Wolverhampton Wanderers at Selhurst Park in the first leg of their semi-final. The first half finished goalless, but Neil Shipperley put the hosts ahead midway through the second half with a header. With a minute remaining, Dougie Freedman scored with a strike from 25 yards out to double the lead. Jamie Smith pulled one back almost immediately, but in a crazy end to the game, Freedman then scored his second with a chip over Mike Stowell in the Wolves goal to secure a 3-1 aggregate lead. The second leg came four days later, and Mark Atkins put the home side ahead after half an hour with a low shot through Palace keeper Carlo Nash's legs. David Hopkin equalised midway through the second half before Ady Williams made it 2-1 to Wolves with five minutes left. There were to be no further goals, however, and Crystal Palace progressed to the final with a 4-3 win on aggregate.

Sheffield United welcomed Ipswich Town to Bramall Lane on 10 May for their first leg, and took the lead in the 40th minute when Jan Åge Fjørtoft shot past Richard Wright in the Ipswich goal. With 12 minutes remaining, Mike Stockwell took advantage of a defensive mix-up to shoot into an empty net and, with that, the night ended 1-1. The return leg at Portman Road took place four days later; Pyotr Kachuro put Sheffield United ahead with a shot that hit the underside of the bar before it was adjudged to have crossed the goal line. James Scowcroft levelled the tie in the 32nd minute with a header before Niklas Gudmundsson gave Ipswich the lead in the 73rd minute. That advantage lasted for just four minutes as Andy Walker made it 2-2, the final score. With the scores level at 3-3 on aggregate, the game carried on with extra time, but neither side could be separated so the Blades progressed on the away goals rule.

Whether anyone had expected the 1997 final to be between Sheffield United and Crystal Palace was certainly up for debate. Both sides had eliminated the teams that had finished above them, but the final points totals of all the play-off sides suggested a far closer affair than many may have anticipated. With that, there was little to separate the two teams and the only goal of the game arrived right at the death. Dean Gordon's shot from just outside the box was deflected out of play by Carl Tiler, resulting in a corner. Simon Rodger floated the cross, which was cleared by Tiler, but it fell to Hopkin, who struck the ball into the top corner from 25 yards out. The referee's whistle followed soon afterwards and Crystal Palace were promoted to the Premier League.

In a bid to remain in the top flight, Palace spent big in the summer transfer window. Italian midfielder Attilio Lombardo was the headline signing and one of the most famous names to wear a Palace shirt when he arrived at Selhurst Park. The former Juventus man was signed for £1.6m alongside Kevin Miller for £1.5m from Watford, Itzik Zohar for £1.2m from Beitar Jerusalem, and Wolves duo Neil Emblen and Jamie Smith for £2m and £1m respectively.

The signings had looked like they might secure Palace's Premier League status as they sat tenth by late November. They had enjoyed mid-table form through the opening third of the season, but from the end of November they struggled. After their victory over Tottenham on 24 November, the Eagles won just a further three times while taking only another five points from draws. The 16 losses they had suffered in a run of 24 games had condemned them to the foot of the table, and Palace were relegated back to the First Division.

* * *

Season 1997/98

First Division play-off final

25 May 1998

Charlton Athletic 4 (Mendonca 23, 71, 103; Rufus 85)

Sunderland 4 (Quinn 50, 73; Phillips 58; Summerbee 99)

(After extra time; Charlton win 7-6 on penalties)

A new television deal had been agreed for the Premier League before the 1997/98 season. After the popularity of football had risen in the United Kingdom, helped mainly by the improvement of safety at family-friendly grounds since the disasters and trouble in the 1980s and England's successful staging of UEFA Euro 96, Sky renewed their deal with the Premier League for £607m. The contract had come over a shortened four-year period compared to the five agreed for the inaugural season, but it was just short of double the value of the previous one per season.

Charlton had played in the second tier since their relegation from the then First Division at the end of the 1989/90 season, which had been one of consistently bad form and the lack of inspiration to change that meant they picked up just seven wins.

The following 1990/91 season had seen Charlton finish 16th in the Second Division. They had won 13, drawn 17 and lost 16, but they made a huge improvement in 1991/92. The Addicks lost just once in their opening six games before facing back-to-back defeats shortly after. Their good form had returned when they took 17 points from their next seven games but, after seeing that run ended, winning didn't return straight away. From the end of November until the beginning of March, Charlton's form was mixed. They won six, drew two and lost six before finding some form at the right time. Following their defeat to Grimsby Town on 3 March, they went unbeaten, winning six and drawing four before they faced back-to-back defeats to end their season.

They had had a huge opportunity to secure promotion back to the top division, but it wasn't to be; the end of 1991/92 had seen them finish seventh and three points outside the play-offs. That was followed by finishes of 11th, 12th and 15th over the next three campaigns, but 1995/96 marked a change for Charlton. Alan Curbishley was made sole manager and had the team in the play-offs at the end of the season after finishing sixth.

Charlton were eliminated at the semi-final stage, losing to south London rivals Crystal

Palace, and found the following season tough. A disappointing 15th-placed finish came in 1996/97 before Curbishley led Charlton to the play-offs once more. The Addicks won 26 of their 46 games, enjoying lengthy runs of good form which carried them into fourth place, enough to see them face Ipswich Town in the semi-finals while Sunderland battled Sheffield United in the other tie.

Portman Road was the venue for the first leg between Charlton and Ipswich Town and an early own goal from Jamie Clapham was the only goal of an ill-disciplined match; tempers flared after the final whistle. The second leg took place at The Valley just three days later, and again the Londoners won 1-0. Ipswich dominated parts of the second half but didn't create too much in the way of chances, forcing just one save from Saša Ilić.

Sunderland travelled to Bramall Lane and had taken an early lead through Kevin Ball in their first leg. The opening goal came in the 17th minute before Marcelo equalised for the hosts, then Vasilios Borbokis netted the winner with 15 minutes left to give Sheffield United a 2-1 lead into the second leg. The return came three days later with Sunderland taking the lead again: Nicky Marker deflected a cross-shot from Allan Johnston past his own keeper midway through the first half. Their lead was doubled in the 38th minute as Kevin Phillips scored just before the break. Lionel Pérez made two saves to deny Graham Stuart before keeping Paul Devlin's shot out, helping the Black Cats to a 2-0 win and a 3-2 victory on aggregate.

The final took place on 25 May at Wembley, and it was Charlton who drew first blood midway through the first half as Clive Mendonca struck a shot past Pérez. Sunderland had had opportunities to find a way back at the end of the half but equalised at the start of the second.

Niall Quinn scored the goal, and the equaliser had swung the game in Sunderland's favour as they took the lead through Phillips, but Mendonca scored his second with around 70 minutes on the clock to bring the game back level. Sunderland's lead was then restored two minutes later before Richard Rufus headed in at the end of the 90 minutes to make it 3-3.

Extra time had kept up with the theme of the match with Sunderland retaking the lead; Nicky Summerbee struck a shot from the edge of the box to make it 4-3, before Steve Jones played the ball behind for Mendonca, who volleyed past Pérez for his third of the afternoon to level the game for a fourth time. The teams couldn't be separated, and penalties were needed to decide a winner. The first penalty was scored by Mendonca before Summerbee, Brown, Johnston, Keith Jones, Ball, Kinsella, Makin, Bowen and Rae all successfully dispatched from the spot to make it 5-5. Robinson and Quinn both scored to make it 6-6 before Shaun Newton stepped up to give Charlton the advantage. Gray's weak shot was then saved by Ilić and the match was won by the Addicks, who returned to the top flight.

Charlton Athletic had made a good start to their Premier League campaign but their form soon dipped; after losing lost just three of their opening 13 games, they picked up just one point in the ten that followed. They were the final side to face relegation from the Premier League at the end of the 1998/99 season after a late revival by Southampton.

* * *

Season 1998/99

First Division play-off final

31 May 1999

Bolton Wanderers 0

Watford 2 (Wright 38; Smart 89)

Life was good for Watford under the management of Graham Taylor. Having previously managed the club between 1977 and 1987, he returned for a second spell ahead of the 1997/98 season. Under his leadership, Watford secured the Second Division title, beating Bristol City to top spot after a season-long battle. The Hornets had enjoyed a fruitful campaign, claiming 88 points with 24 wins and 16 draws but, more notably, they had only lost six times.

They found it tougher at the higher level, losing five times by 17 October before going on to lose another six times between late December and early March. The losses didn't define their season; they went ten games unbeaten on two separate occasions in 1998/99, seeing them race to a fifth-placed finish.

It was Birmingham City in the play-off semi-final for Watford. The Blues had finished four points ahead of Taylor's team, but with the first leg being played at Vicarage Road, the Hornets knew they could take full advantage. It was a win for the Hertfordshire club with the only goal coming in the fifth minute, Michel Ngonge heading in Peter Kennedy's cross. In the second leg four days later, Dele Adebola opened the scoring for Birmingham after just two minutes, levelling the tie at 1-1 on aggregate. The hosts' task to progress to the final was made tougher despite being at home as David Holdsworth received a second yellow card with more than an hour left to play. The ten men managed to hold on for the rest of regular time and through extra time as penalties were needed to settle the tie. At 6-6, with one spot kick missed by each team, Watford's Alon Hazan put them ahead before Chris Holland's miss condemned Birmingham to defeat.

Bolton Wanderers faced Ipswich Town at home in their first leg with the first half ending goalless. The only goal of the game came six minutes from time when Michael Johansen volleyed the ball into the Ipswich net. The second leg at Portman Road came three days later and Ipswich took the lead 14 minutes in with Matt Holland scoring. Bob Taylor levelled with a close-range effort before Ipswich were ahead once again one minute later through Kieron Dyer, but a deflected strike by Per Frandsen made the score level again with seven minutes remaining. Dyer then netted his second of the game, scoring with a header to make it 3-2 to Ipswich and level the tie on aggregate. With extra time needed, Taylor also scored his second and Bolton's third in the 96th minute before Holland's 20-yard strike made it 4-3 to Ipswich in the 116th minute. Although they had won on the night, with the tie level at 4-4 on aggregate, Bolton progressed to the final through the away goals rule.

The final came on 31 May and Bolton dominated the early stages, but the opening goal went the way of Watford. Described as one of the best goals seen in a play-off final, Nick Wright scored an overhead kick after the ball had fallen to him from a Neil Cox headed clearance. It remained 1-0 until the 89th minute when Watford doubled their lead: Peter Kennedy won the ball from Scott Sellars and passed it to Allan Smart who slotted it beyond Bolton keeper Steve Banks. Their 2-0 win had secured back-to-back promotions for Watford and their place in the top flight.

Watford had had some encouraging early results in the Premier League with victories over Liverpool and Chelsea but, despite having an experienced manager in Graham Taylor, they largely struggled. Three of their six wins came in the opening eight games of the season, seeing the Hornets sit mid-table before they dropped into the relegation zone with a 3-1 loss at home to Middlesbrough on 24 October and remained there until the end of the season. Watford's season isn't considered one of the worst in Premier League history, despite the club only winning 24 points with six wins and six draws.

* * *

Season 1999/2000

First Division play-off final

29 May 2000

Barnsley 2 (Wright 6 og; Hignett 78 pen)

Ipswich Town 4 (Mowbray 28; Naylor 52; Stewart 58; Reuser 90)

Neither Barnsley nor Ipswich Town had ever been in the First Division play-off final. The Yorkshire side had been relegated from the Premier League at the end of the 1997/98 season with a 19th-place finish and had followed that up with a 13th-placed finish in the First Division, but Ipswich had spent a decade and a half in the second tier after their relegation from the top flight at the end of the 1994/95 season.

After finishing bottom of the table that year, Ipswich had not fallen below the top ten in the First Division as they sought a place back in the Premier League. Manager George Burley had come into the job on 28 December 1994 and, with a record of four wins, two draws and 16 defeats, he wasn't able to save Ipswich from their doomed fate. He remained in charge going into 1995/96 and found his side immediately challenging for a return to the big league. A mixed campaign had seen them finish seventh and narrowly miss out on the play-offs by two points but, with Burley remaining in charge, Ipswich got better.

They sat in the bottom half of the table for most of the first half of 1996/97 but their form improved in the new year. A ten-game unbeaten run had seen them move into the play-off spots before they cemented their place there with a six-game unbeaten run at the end of the season. They fell short against Sheffield United in the semi-finals, however, drawing in both legs but losing out on the away goals rule.

During the 1997/98 season, Ipswich also saw some big changes to their squad. Tony Vaughan had been sold to Manchester City for £1.35m while Craig Forrest and Steve Sedgley both moved for £500,000, to West Ham United and Wolverhampton Wanderers respectively. In their place Ipswich had signed Matt Holland from Bournemouth for £800,000, Mark Venus from Wolves for £150,000 and Jamie Clapham from Spurs for £300,000, as well as Lee Bracey and David Johnson from Bury with that latter signing costing £1.1m.

The East Anglian side fell short again in the 1997 play-offs. They hadn't made the best start to the season, winning just six games and losing eight times by late December. Their fortunes changed after Boxing Day as they lost just once in a run of 23, with their impressive record carrying them to a fifth-placed finish. The week's gap between their final game of the season and their first leg with Charlton Athletic hadn't proved beneficial as they went down 1-0 to the Addicks before losing to them by the same scoreline in the second leg and their promotion hopes were ended.

It was the same story for Ipswich in 1998/99 too. After an impressive run saw them finish third, they were defeated in the play-off semi-finals against Bolton Wanderers on the away goals rule after drawing 4-4 on aggregate.

Burley hadn't given up hope of bringing Ipswich back to the top flight and 1999/2000 had given them their fourth opportunity to win the play-offs, but it could have been very different. On the final day of the season, with Ipswich beating Walsall 1-0 and second-placed Manchester City trailing Blackburn, the Tractor Boys briefly sat in the automatic promotion spots. David Johnson added a second in that game but Manchester City eventually scored four, bumping Burley's team down to third place.

Bolton, hoping for a different ending from their Wembley loss in 1999, were Ipswich's opponents for the semi-finals. It had looked like an uphill battle for Ipswich when they found themselves 2-0 down, Dean Holdsworth and Eiður Guðjohnsen scoring in the fifth and 26th minutes respectively. The Suffolk side battled their way back into the tie with Marcus Stewart volleying the ball past Jussi Jääskeläinen before hc added a second in the 65th minute. With the first leg ending level, it was all to play for in the second at

Portman Road, where Bolton took an early lead again through Holdsworth before Jim Magilton equalised from the penalty spot. The Wanderers retook the lead just before half-time when Holdsworth scored with a magnificent free kick, before a goal for either side after the break came minutes apart: Magilton got his and Town's second when he beat two defenders and drove the ball high into the net before Allan Johnston swiftly scored a volley to put Bolton back ahead. The scoring hadn't finished there; with time slipping away from Ipswich, Magilton notched his hat-trick in the dying minutes to send the tie to extra time where they booked their place at Wembley. Jamie Clapham scored from the penalty spot before Martijn Reuser added a fifth to send Burley's team through.

With Ipswich and Barnsley scoring 12 times between them over two legs, many had expected there to be goals at Wembley, and they weren't disappointed. Barnsley took the lead in the sixth minute when Richard Wright scored an own goal after Craig Hignett's effort rebounded off the crossbar and off the arm of the goalkeeper into the back of the net. Ipswich equalised midway through the first half with a goal from Tony Mowbray before they added another two six minutes apart, a third of the way through the second period: Marcus Stewart played a long ball into Richard Naylor who passed it beyond Kevin Miller, before Stewart headed in a cross from Clapham.

Barnsley were awarded a penalty in the 77th minute after Mowbray was adjudged to have fouled Geoff Thomas with Hignett converting from 12 yards. Barnsley committed players forward in search of a late equaliser, and the tie was settled in the final minute of the game: Reuser picked up the ball in his own half, ran half the length of the pitch and struck his shot from the edge of the box into the roof of the net to confirm Ipswich's return to the Premier League.

Ipswich weren't backed by many to remain in the top flight after the 2000/01 season but surprised their critics when they were challenging for a top-six spot. Burley kept much of the squad that had won the club promotion, making Reuser's loan from Ajax permanent for £1m as well as adding Hermann Hreiðarsson from Wimbledon for a fee of around £4m. For much of the campaign it had looked like Ipswich would finish in the top three, but a 2-1 defeat at Charlton had ended any hopes of that with two games left and they ended up in fifth place.

The following year didn't go as well, however, as Ipswich fell victim to the so-called second-season syndrome. They had brought in Pablo Couñago, Andy Marshall, Tommy Miller, Finidi George, Matteo Sereni and Thomas

Gaardsøe for a combined £9.35m but it didn't stop them having a dismal start. Ipswich won just once in their opening 18 games, leaving them in the relegation zone before a patch of form between late December and February moved them up to 12th. It had looked like that would be enough for survival but another slump with just six points in 13 games condemned them to a return to the First Division.

* * *

Matt Holland had joined Ipswich ahead of the 1997/98 season, and contributed ten goals in 46 games to the 1999/2000 promotion cause. I spoke to him about the club's rise to the top flight.

You signed for Ipswich for a fee of £800,000 in 1997. What enticed you to join the club?

MH: At the time it was a no-brainer for me. I was at Bournemouth, who were in financial trouble and needed to sell an asset. They had

had a few offers for me, and I was ambitious, wanting to play at the highest-possible level, so for a team in a higher division coming in for me and had just been in the play-offs, it was quite an easy decision.

As you've mentioned, the club had featured in the play-offs the season before you joined. Was there an emphasis on achieving the same target while you were at Ipswich?

MH: I don't know if there was an emphasis on what we needed to achieve, but we understood where we were in the league and what we wanted to achieve: getting back into the Premier League. The club had been there in 1992 and had been relegated a couple of years later so we just wanted to get back there as soon as possible.

You beat Barnsley 4-2 in the final to seal promotion. How tough is it to play in a play-off final knowing what is up for grabs?

MH: I will go as far as saying it is the most pressurised game I have ever played in, and I played in the Premier League and at a World Cup but, for me, there is no game quite like it. You know what the prize is, you know what is at stake, and we had been so close so many times, we certainly felt the pressure more than most. There's always a sense of relief when the final whistle goes but the overwhelming feeling when you do achieve promotion is a sense of pride.

In their first season back in the Premier League, Ipswich were one of the favourites to be relegated, but defied the odds to survive before facing the drop the following year. Are players always aware of these opinions before a season and how does that help spur you on?

MH: I think when you go up, especially through the play-offs, I think there's just an expectation for you to go straight back down. We were certainly aware of that fact, but we had a belief among the squad that we could compete, and I think you're never quite sure how it'd go because not everyone in the squad would have experienced playing in the Premier League. When we drew with Manchester United [at Portman Road, in their second match of the season], a side who had recently won the treble, it gave everyone the belief we could compete with anybody.

The 2000s

Season 2000/01

First Division play-off final

28 May 2001

Bolton Wanderers 3 (Farrelly 17; Ricketts 89; Gardner 90)

Preston North End 0

AN IMMEDIATE return to the Premier League had been scuppered by Watford in the 1999 play-off final but Bolton had had another opportunity the following season. The club had made an early change in their managerial hot seat with Colin Todd resigning seven games into 1999/2000 after the sale of Per Frandsen to Blackburn Rovers. Under Todd, Wanderers had won just once in those opening games before Phil Brown took charge on an interim basis for a month. Brown had seen the team lose just once in his very short tenure before Sam Allardyce was made manager in October.

While Bolton had enjoyed mostly good form under Allardyce, they did have a patch of form that had seen them pick up just three points in a run of seven games, but it wasn't enough to derail their season as they finished sixth and qualified for the play-offs again. Their run had ended at the hands of Ipswich Town in the semi-final, losing 7-5 on aggregate. It was another difficult season for Bolton, who had missed another chance at promotion, but there was always 2000/01.

With Allardyce still at the helm, Bolton enjoyed another good campaign. They lost just a handful of times, with five of their seven defeats coming before the new year. Their impressive form saw them finish third, joined by Preston North End, Birmingham City and West Bromwich Albion in the play-offs, with Bolton facing West Brom and Preston going up against Birmingham.

Bolton travelled to The Hawthorns on 13 May and the match was dominated by the hosts, but it wasn't until a minute before half-time that they took the lead when Jason Roberts ran on to a Richard Sneekes pass and struck the ball past Matt Clarke in the Bolton goal. Ten minutes into the second half, Colin Hendry brought Roberts down, conceding a penalty which was converted by Lee Hughes to make it 2-0. Guðni Bergsson reduced the deficit in the final ten minutes with a header before Bolton were awarded a penalty in the 88th minute after Tony Butler fouled Bo Hansen. Per Frandsen converted and the match finished

2-2. The second leg came four days later with Bolton sealing a 3-0 win: Bergsson opened the scoring after ten minutes, converting a free kick from Simon Charlton, before the lead was doubled in the 63rd minute through Ricardo Gardner, and a last-minute goal from Michael Ricketts secured the victory.

In Birmingham, after a goalless first half, Nicky Eaden put the Blues ahead in the 54th minute. That was the only goal of the game, and the second leg followed at Deepdale four days later. The opening goal in Lancashire came midway through the first half when David Healy struck the ball high into the Birmingham net to level the aggregate score. With an hour played, Geoff Horsfield gave Birmingham the overall lead in the tie, converting Stan Lazaridis's cross at the far post. Preston's Graham Alexander saw his spot kick in the 78th minute rattle the bar before Birmingham conceded a last-minute goal from Mark Rankine, making it 2-2 on aggregate and sending the tie into extra time. There were no more goals, so it was a penalty shoot-out to settle the team facing Bolton in the final. Marcelo and Purse both missed for Birmingham and despite Preston's Rob Edwards seeing his effort go awry, Paul McKenna's effort ensured that North End won 4-2.

The 2001 final was the first to be played away from Wembley since 1989, back in the days when the final was contested over two legs. Bolton and Preston fans descended on the Welsh capital Cardiff, seeking a place in the Premier League. Preston dominated the early stages but Bolton took the lead in the 17th minute. A long free kick wasn't cleared and allowed Gareth Farrelly to shoot from just outside the box and past David Lucas. The scoreline remained unchanged until the final moments of the game when Ricketts doubled Bolton's lead as the forward rounded the keeper and passed the ball into an empty net. A minute later, Gardner wrapped it up; he dispossessed Alexander in the Bolton half, went beyond a tired Colin Murdock and slotted the ball home to secure Wanderers' promotion to the top flight.

Bolton had only been in the Premier League for two seasons before 2001/02, facing immediate relegation on both occasions, but this time it was different. They stayed up in 16th and 17th over the next two years and then kicked on. Wanderers hadn't spent a lot of money in their first four seasons back in the Premier League, spending a total of around £4m, before their spending increased as the years went on. Four top-ten finishes between 2003/04 and 2006/07 had been good, but by the 2007/08 season Bolton found themselves dropping down the table. Their spending didn't stop there, spending £17.3m and £18m in 2007/08 and 2008/09 but getting finishes of 16th and 13th for their troubles. The next two seasons saw them finish 14th, before they were relegated at the end of the 2011/12 season, despite spending another £13m.

* * *

Season 2001/02

First Division play-off final

12 May 2002

Birmingham City 1 (Horsfield 102)

Norwich City 1 (Roberts 91)

(After extra time; Birmingham win 4-2 on penalties)

The old Wembley had shut its doors for the final time in October 2000, making way for the new stadium that would be built in its place. Ipswich Town had beaten Barnsley 4-2 in the last First Division play-off final to secure promotion to the Premier League, with the Millennium Stadium in Cardiff taking over the hosting of the match until the new stadium opened.

Birmingham had missed out on the 1998 play-offs after a seventh-place finish. Their season had started well with the Blues taking 13 points from their opening five games. After sitting second in the league following those five games, their form dropped and they managed just one win between mid-September and late November before winning 14, drawing ten and losing three through until the end of the season as they clawed their way back towards the play-offs. Birmingham had finished level on points with Sheffield United, who took the final play-off spot having scored nine more goals than the men from St Andrew's.

The 1998/99 season was an improvement, but in the play-offs Birmingham fell short when losing to Watford in the semi-finals. There wasn't much in the way of bad form for the Blues throughout the campaign, with the worst run being a three-game losing streak, but they had quickly recovered from that. From late September to April, Birmingham had gone on three separate eight-game unbeaten runs, launching them towards the play-offs.

The disappointment that came with defeat to the Hornets had to be put in the back of the minds of the Birmingham players as they looked upon the new season, in which they finished fifth but lost in the play-off semi-final again, as they then did in 2000/01.

The Blues sat top of the First Division by the end of September 1999, losing just once in their opening nine games. Their form had dropped between October and late December, seeing them dwindle around mid-table before they slowly clawed their way back towards the play-offs where they couldn't reduce the deficit from the first leg, losing 4-0 to Barnsley and only winning 2-1 at Oakwell, with the Tykes going on to lose to Ipswich at Wembley.

After winning just one of their opening three games and finding themselves 14th in 2000/01, Birmingham's form improved, and they sat in the play-off places for the rest of the season. The Blues bounced between second and sixth until May, all but confirming a final fifth-place finish with a goalless draw at Burnley on 21 April. For a third year in a row, the Midlands side had hoped to progress to the play-off final and, after a 1-0 win in the first leg, Birmingham lost 2-1 to Preston at Deepdale before going out on penalties to the Lancashire side.

A third consecutive loss in the play-off semi-final had taken its toll on Birmingham, but they had still gone into the 2001/02 season hopeful of finally achieving promotion to the Premier League. However, their start to the campaign had been dismal. Four wins, two draws and four losses did see the Blues rise to third in the table before rapidly dropping to 14th. They added two more draws at the end of September before beating Barnsley 3-1 on the road, but it wasn't enough to keep Trevor Francis in a job. The Birmingham manager had been dismissed midway through October. Mick Mills and Jim Barron had been made caretaker managers, taking charge of the club until 12 December when Steve Bruce was brought in. Under the management of Mills and Barron, they had won five, drew four and lost three.

A defeat to Wolverhampton Wanderers in the first game in charge for Bruce had seen the team sit tenth, but they soon started to climb the table. The improvement from mid-December to the end of the season saw Birmingham climb to fifth, qualifying for the play-offs for a fourth consecutive year. With their final position confirmed, the Blues faced Millwall in the semi-final, with Wolverhampton Wanderers taking on Norwich City.

There was very little to separate Birmingham and Millwall in the first leg at St Andrew's. After a goalless first half, Bryan Hughes scored early in the second period to put the hosts ahead, but with 11 minutes remaining the London side had pulled it back level: Dion Dublin, who was on loan from the Blues' rivals Aston Villa, headed in a Steven Reid cross and the match finished 1-1. The sides met again four days later at The Den and, like the first leg, there was little difference between the teams. The game remained goalless until the final minute when a shot across the Millwall box by Steve Vickers was put into the net by Stern John, winning the tie for Birmingham.

Wolves had travelled to Carrow Road for the opening leg of their semi-final with Norwich and it was no surprise that they took the lead after a positive start, Dean Sturridge putting them ahead midway through the first half. From there it was all Norwich. Mark Rivers levelled the tie in the 56th minute with a volley before further goals from Paul McVeigh and Malky Mackay secured a 3-1 victory for the hosts. The return leg came three days later, and Wolves fancied their chances of overturning their two-goal deficit. There was nothing in the way of goals in the first half and the only goal of the game came in the 76th minute when Kevin Cooper's strike from 35 yards out nestled into the net. Wolves won on the night, but it was Norwich who progressed to the final with a 3-2 win on aggregate.

Tension was high in Cardiff with neither Birmingham nor Norwich having ever featured in the second-tier play-off final before and the nervousness showed as the match finished 0-0. It went to extra time and Norwich were ahead within the first minute after Iwan Roberts headed in an Alex Notman cross. That lead only lasted for 11 minutes as Birmingham found an equaliser in the 102nd minute. Jeff Kenna had crossed for Stern John, who helped the ball back across goal. Rob Green was left stranded with Geoff Horsfield heading in at the back post. No more goals followed in the second half of extra time, and penalties decided the winner. Roberts took the first and scored before John levelled. Paul Devlin made it 2-1 to Birmingham, either side of misses for Philip Mulryne and Daryl Sutch. After Stan Lazaridis had scored his attempt, Clint Easton added to the tally, but Darren Carter secured victory for Bruce's team with his penalty.

Following their promotion to the Premier League, Birmingham spent a total of four seasons in the top flight. They finished mid-table with successive positions of 13th, tenth and 12th, before relegation at the end of the

2005/06 season, finishing 18th. Over those four campaigns the Blues picked up an equal share of the £1.1bn paid by Sky for TV rights, earning themselves just over £18m per season. An EU ruling had cut the length of their rights offer, reducing it to a three-year cycle, but the television giant still broadcast over 190 games across the contracted years.

***

Season 2002/03

First Division play-off final

26 May 2003

Sheffield United 0

Wolverhampton Wanderers 3
(Kennedy 6; Blake 22; Miller 45)

The 2000/01 season for Wolves had produced their lowest finish for five seasons. Following their loss in the 1996/97 play-off semi-final, the West Midlands side still had ambitions of promotion. Their third-place finish had been followed by placings of ninth, seventh, seventh and 12th, and something needed to change if they were to reach the Premier League.

Over the course of the 2001/02 season, Wolves spent in excess of £11m, with around £7.3m spent in the summer alone. They brought in Mark Kennedy (Manchester City), Shaun Newton (Charlton Athletic), Colin Cameron (Hearts), Nathan Blake (Blackburn Rovers) and Alex Rae (Sunderland) to strengthen the squad and it almost worked. They had sat in the automatic promotion spots for the majority of the campaign, but a late slump in form, with them winning just two of their final nine games, had seen West Bromwich Albion pip them to second place.

Finishing third place had given them a second chance at promotion, but those hopes were ended by Norwich City in the semi-final. After losing 3-1 at Carrow Road, a 1-0 win at home wasn't enough to see them through to the Millennium Stadium. The club knew they were almost there in their pursuit of Premier League promotion, but they hadn't spent much during the summer, although the players they had brought in included former England captain Paul Ince and ex-Manchester United stalwart Denis Irwin.

The start of 2002/03 had seen Wolves sit in the automatic promotion spots after going unbeaten in their first five matches, but they dropped to mid-table after a bad run. Their good form returned towards the end of October until mid-December, but they took a hit once again over the Christmas period. In the second half of the season, Wolves only lost a further two times in a run of 21 games with their impressive form carrying them up the table and into the play-offs.

Wolves welcomed fourth-placed Reading to Molineux for the first leg of their semi-final, but it was the visitors who took the lead when midway through the first half Nicky Forster converted a cross from Nicky Shorey. The equaliser came from second-half substitute Shaun Newton after he struck a shot past Marcus Hahnemann in the Reading goal. The scores remained level until the 84th minute with the hosts taking the lead with a free kick from Lee Naylor and the match ended 2-1. The sides met again four days later, and it was Wolves who came away victorious. The only goal arrived via Alex Rae's 15-yard effort and gave Wolves a 3-1 win on aggregate.

Their opponents would be either Sheffield United or Nottingham Forest, who went through a goalless first half in the first leg at the City Ground, but ten minutes into the second half David Johnson latched on to a deflected pass from Andy Reid and scored past Paddy Kenny to put the hosts ahead. The lead only lasted for two minutes as Michael Brown scored a penalty after he had been brought down. With the tie level going into the second leg, Johnson opened the scoring after half an hour following a defensive error by John Curtis before their lead was doubled in the 58th minute with a volley from Reid. The Blades responded almost immediately with Brown scoring, and then had their equaliser eight minutes later with Steven Kabba striking an effort from 15 yards out. The teams remained unseparated after two legs of football and extra time was needed to settle the tie. Paul Peschisolido made it 3-2 in the 112th minute before Des Walker's own goal was United's fourth of the night, making it 5-3 on aggregate. Rob Page scored a very late own goal too, but Sheffield United progressed to the final, winning 5-4 on aggregate.

The finalists met in Cardiff on 26 May 2003, and it didn't take Wolves long to open the scoring, Mark Kennedy getting them on their way with a low drive into the corner. Colin Cameron's shot was then deflected behind by Paddy Kenny with Nathan Blake heading in the resulting corner to double the lead in the 22nd minute, and they had a third just before half-time when Kenny Miller converted a cross from Newton. There was no fightback from Sheffield United and Wolves secured their place in the top flight for the first time in 20 years.

The 2003/04 season marked Wolves' first appearance in the newly founded Premier League, but their return to the top tier was short-lived. The team struggled throughout the campaign, winning just seven times and spending the majority of the season in the relegation zone, and they ended up finishing bottom. Their relegation was effectively confirmed after they failed to win their penultimate game against Newcastle United, drawing 1-1 at St James' Park, as their inferior goal difference meant it would've been a miracle had Wolves stayed up. Although they had won on 1 May 2004 at home to Everton, relegation rivals Manchester City beating Newcastle effectively ruled out their survival.

* * *

Season 2003/04

First Division play-off final

29 May 2004

Crystal Palace 1 (Shipperley 62)

West Ham United 0

Crystal Palace had started the 2003/04 season well, winning their first three games and sitting top of the table, but that was as good as it got under manager Steve Kember. Between late August and the start of November, the Eagles then only won once, beating Cardiff City at Selhurst Park. The 5-0 loss to Wigan Athletic on 1 November was chairman Simon Jordan's last straw as he let Kember go with Kit Symons taking over as caretaker manager before the permanent appointment of Iain Dowie just before Christmas.

Three wins, three draws and two losses had seen Symonds steady the ship and despite his replacement losing his first game in charge on Boxing Day, Dowie's influence on the team propelled them into the play-offs, finishing sixth behind Sunderland, West Ham United and Ipswich Town. Their final league position meant they faced third-placed Sunderland in the semi-final while West Ham were pitted against Ipswich.

A goalless first half between Palace and Sunderland was followed by the latter taking the lead early in the second half through a Marcus Stewart penalty. The floodgates then opened and within a minute Shipperley equalised with a header before Danny Butterfield's deflected shot gave Palace the lead ten minutes later. The scoring continued as the match approached its end: Kevin Kyle levelled the tie in the 85th minute before Andrew Johnson restored Palace's lead two minutes later, giving them a 3-2 win on the day. The second leg came three days later at the Stadium of Light with Kyle levelling on aggregate in the 42nd minute and Stewart scoring a header just before half-time to make it 4-3 to Sunderland overall. Darren Powell's header made it 4-4 on aggregate later in the match and sent the tie to penalties. John Oster and Jason McAteer both missed for Sunderland while Mart Poom saved from Shaun Derry and Wayne Routledge. Jeff Whitley then failed to score his spot kick and Michael Hughes struck the winning penalty.

West Ham's first leg at Portman Road had also had a goalless first half. The only goal of the match came 12 minutes into the second half with Darren Bent scoring a header after Richard Naylor's initial effort had rebounded off the crossbar. The Boleyn Ground hosted the second leg three days later and after yet another goalless first half, the opening goal arrived in the 50th minute as Matthew Etherington scored from inside the Ipswich penalty area with a goal described as 'a screamer' to level the tie. Twelve minutes later, it was 2-0 when an Etherington corner was defended poorly by Ipswich, and Christian Dailly's shot was deflected into the goal to give West Ham a 2-1 aggregate win and a place in the final.

The two London sides descended on the Welsh capital, but the game was far from a classic. Missed chances for both teams meant the first half finished goalless before West Ham increased the pressure early in the second half. However, the deadlock was broken in the 62nd minute by the Eagles as Shipperley scored. Johnson twisted and struck a shot through Dailly's legs, then Stephen Bywater had failed to hold the shot, allowing the Palace forward to tap home from close range. The east Londoners had had their chances to equalise, but Palace held on and secured promotion to the Premier League.

In the top flight, Crystal Palace struggled for form. Their opening seven games saw them take just two points with five losses sandwiched between two draws. The rest of the season had seen the Eagles win seven, draw ten and lose 14 and, while they remained just ahead of the relegation zone for most of the run-in, a 2-2 draw with Charlton and a win for West Brom over Portsmouth saw the Selhurst Park team relegated on the final day.

* * *

Danny Butterfield had scored four goals during the 2003/04 season as well as an important one during the semi-final first leg. I spoke to him about Crystal Palace's promotion to the Premier League.

When you first joined Crystal Palace in 2002, was there ever any talk about achieving promotion to the Premier League?

DB: I joined Palace from Grimsby, who I felt were always punching above their weight, and Crystal Palace were always a team that finished in the top ten. My ambitions were to be fighting for a team that was in the shape for play-offs and promotion. Simon Jordan certainly had ambitions to get there and was slowly but surely building a squad to achieve that and I felt it was better to be playing for a team that was higher up the league.

In your first season, Palace finished 14th before going on to finish sixth in 2003/04. What changes were made to improve the club's fortunes?

DB: The club went from having players who were experienced and had had a fantastic career to having a squad with a lot of players who needed to prove themselves. It was a good mix to have among the squad and the confidence certainly grew when Iain Dowie came in.

You scored in the semi-final first leg and Palace won that game 3-2. Did you feel that performance alone was good enough to make the final or did you feel there was a lot of work still to do?

DB: The play-offs are such a lottery and you usually found that around that era, play-off semi-finals were very high-scoring. Teams would go into the first legs and attack to try and get leads so it almost always became a basketball match at times, as opposed to it being cagey and tactical.

We had an incredible belief and just felt it was our time, especially with the confidence we had carried all season from being in the bottom three at Christmas to making the play-offs.

After beating Sunderland on penalties, you faced West Ham United in the final. It worked out in a way where the Hammers had more of the ball, but Crystal Palace still managed to get the win. How tough is it sitting back and then trying to get forward with limited opportunities?

DB: The goal we scored gave us even more confidence that it was our day and when you've got a one-goal lead to defend, it gives you an extra 15 per cent in determination and grit. There was a lot riding on the game, but I think we were so determined to keep the ball out of the net, I think that was what got us over the line.

* * *

Season 2004/05

Championship play-off final

30 May 2005

Preston North End 0

West Ham United 1 (Zamora 57)

The First Division was rebranded as the Championship ahead of the 2004/05 season as a way to boost the popularity of England's Football League. Its previous name had existed since 1888, ending 116 years of history.

Ten years in the top flight for West Ham had come to an end in 2003. They had finished seventh in the Premier League in 2001/02 and hopes remained high for their young squad to expand on this, aiming for an equal or higher finish in the 2002/03 season. They had boasted the likes of David James, Trevor Sinclair, Joe Cole, Jermain Defoe, Glen Johnson and Michael Carrick in their ranks but a disastrous start to the season had seen them win just three of their 24 matches, and the Hammers found themselves bottom of the table with just 16 points by Christmas. More poor results followed in the new year, and they continued to struggle in the relegation battle.

When manager Glenn Roeder was taken ill against Middlesbrough in April 2003, it was unclear whether the team's poor form had caused it. Club legend Sir Trevor Brooking was named caretaker manager and with his appointment, West Ham's luck began to change with a series of good results towards the end of the season, leaving them with a chance of staying up. Going into the final day, they were tied on points with Bolton

Wanderers, but far behind on goal difference. They knew they needed a superior result to Bolton to escape relegation. The Wanderers defeated Middlesbrough 2-1, with West Ham's 2-2 draw at Birmingham thanks to goals from Les Ferdinand and Paolo Di Canio confirming their relegation.

After the disappointment of 2003/04 and missing out on an immediate return to the Premier League, the Hammers' 2004/05 season began with four points in the opening two games, but they struggled for consistency and often weren't able to go more than three games unbeaten before facing defeat again. In a run that covered just under half of their season's games, Alan Pardew's West Ham picked up 38 points from the 72 available to them before ending the season with 35 points in 22 games. The Hammers had just one defeat inflicted on them in the final ten, with a run of eight unbeaten, leading them to a sixth-placed finish in the Championship and into play-offs ahead of Reading by three points.

In east London, West Ham welcomed Ipswich Town to the Boleyn Ground for the first leg. Marlon Harewood netted from close range early in the game from a Matthew Etherington cross before the Hammers doubled their lead six minutes later: again, an Etherington cross was delivered but found Bobby Zamora, whose strike beat Kelvin Davis in the Ipswich goal. Just before half-time, the deficit was halved as goalkeeper Jimmy Walker conceded an own goal before Ipswich found an equaliser through Shefki Kuqi, making the most of a defensive mix-up between Walker and Anton Ferdinand, and the match ended 2-2. Portman Road played host to the second leg four days later with the tie still very much in the balance. Zamora scored twice in 11 minutes to put West Ham in control: the first was a close-range header from a Harewood cross before Harewood assisted again as his pass was volleyed into the Ipswich goal, and the Hammers were back in the final.

Preston faced Derby County in their first leg at Deepdale. The home side dominated and took the lead in the 38th minute when David Nugent beat Lee Camp in the Derby goal after picking up a flicked pass from Chris Sedgwick. Although the Rams improved in the second half, it was Preston who scored next, doubling their lead in the final minute of the match with a defensive header deflecting off Richard Cresswell past Camp to make it 2-0 going into the second leg. After a goalless first half at Pride Park Stadium four days later, Grzegorz Rasiak won a late penalty after he was brought down by Chris Lucketti. Rasiak took it himself, but his effort struck a post and the game finished 0-0, with Preston's first-leg win being enough to see them through.

In the final, on 30 May, over 70,000 supporters descended on Cardiff. There was very little between the two sides throughout the game, and the first half ended goalless. Then the crucial moment came just over ten minutes into the second half as Bobby Zamora scored from close range. The ball had been played over to Etherington on the left by Zamora. The favour was returned to the striker and after the beating of Youl Mawéné, he was able to put West Ham ahead with the score remaining that way.

With promotion back to the top flight confirmed, the Hammers remained in the Premier League for six seasons before they went back down again in 2011/12. The 2005/06 season had seen the club finish ninth, though few gave the Hammers much hope of Premier League survival. They surprised many and sat in fourth by the end of October. A run of mediocre form had seen them fall to tenth before they rose back up the table with five straight wins at the start of the new year. A few more good results had seen the east Londoners finish ninth, ahead of Everton, Middlesbrough and Manchester City.

In the other five seasons, West Ham recorded two more top-half finishes, ending up tenth and ninth in 2007/08 and 2008/09 respectively, bookended by 15th in 2006/07 and 17th in 2009/10 before being condemned to a rock-bottom finish in 2011. That season saw West Ham record just one win in their opening 14 games before they recorded only their second win, against Wigan Athletic. They had a run of mixed form between December and March, which was followed by a single point in the final eight games.

* * *

Seven goals in the Championship and four in the play-offs, including the winner against

Preston North End, made Bobby Zamora the perfect person to chat to about West Ham's return to the Premier League.

You joined West Ham after the club had been relegated from the Premier League. When you first signed, was there an ambition to make an immediate return to the top flight?

BZ: Yes. We had a strong side and although a lot of players had left from that relegated side, there was still an ambition to return. I had the opportunity to return to the club that I supported so that was my mindset when I played for the club.

West Ham made the play-offs despite what seemed like a rocky season for the club and came up against Ipswich in the semi-finals. How confident were you going into that game?

BZ: With the play-offs, it's all about momentum. We felt we were in a good place and with clubs that don't get automatic promotion can certainly feel the pressures of the play-offs more than others, but we were on a good run and the changing room when that Ipswich game came around was full of confidence and I think we showed that after the two games.

You dominated the final against Crystal Palace in 2003/04 but lost that game. How tough is it to have such a foothold in the game but not get the desired result?

BZ: It was a disappointing experience for us, but it definitely helped us the following season. To dominate any game and not come away with a win is always disappointing, but more so with the play-off final. It was gutting.

West Ham went through the 2004/05 season without any real lengthy runs of form but still found themselves in the play-offs. What

is it like not having the greatest season, but still finding yourself in the post-season?

BZ: The previous season had been our learning curve. When we reached the play-offs again, we knew exactly what we needed to do to have a different outcome. It certainly made us more relaxed going into that final with Preston. It was a better time as a squad, having had the disappointment of the previous season.

With facing Ipswich again in the semi-final, how tough was it facing them for the second year in a row?

BZ: Ipswich were always one of those sides that I liked to play against. We had played them a few times and had come out on top, so we were positive going into those games. I was pleased to be involved in some of the goals too.

You scored the only goal of the final and sealed West Ham's return to the Premier

League. What did the goal mean to you and what goes through your mind when you've scored the potential winner?

BZ: I remember feeling in control of the game and I don't think there was really any doubt that we wouldn't come away with a win. I didn't hit the ball with the best contact, but it went in and that's all that mattered. I came off with ten or 15 minutes still to go and that was the worst part. Sitting on the bench, with only one goal in it and not being able to influence the game, it's very hard. The boys were fantastic and saw it out for us.

* * *

Season 2005/06

Championship play-off final

21 May 2006

Leeds United 0

Watford 3 (DeMerit 25; Sullivan 57 og; Henderson 84 pen)

Just the previous season, the Hornets had finished 18th in the Championship so any thoughts of them even being in consideration for promotion were scarce. Striker Heiðar Helguson had been sold to Fulham for around £2m, and for a player who scored 16 goals for a side finishing towards the bottom of the table, it was a big loss. His replacement came in the way of Marlon King for £650,000 from League One club Nottingham Forest. The new frontman was crucial in Watford getting promoted against the odds as he netted 21 goals throughout the 2005/06 season, finishing as the Championship's top scorer.

After losing on the opening day, Watford went seven games unbeaten before their worst run of the season came between 17 September and 18 October with just three points in six games.

The Hornets picked up good form once again, winning five and drawing four. One loss in 12 between January and March had seen Watford continue their push towards the play-offs and despite back-to-back losses against Millwall and Crystal Palace, nine points from their final five games propelled them to third place.

The Hertfordshire club faced Crystal Palace in the semi-final, a club they had lost twice to during the season. Watford faced the Eagles at Selhurst Park in the first leg and after a goalless first half, King opened the scoring a minute into the second period. The lead was doubled when Ashley Young curled a free kick into the goal before Matthew Spring scored a third in the 85th minute. The second leg followed three days later but it remained goalless throughout and Watford's 3-0 aggregate score had seen them through.

Leeds welcomed Preston North End to Elland Road in their first leg with the match finishing 1-1. David Nugent gave the visitors the lead in the 48th minute before Eddie Lewis netted the equaliser with a free kick 15 minutes before time. The second leg came three days later at Deepdale where Leeds secured a 2-0 win over the Lilywhites with a header from Rob Hulse and a low strike from Frazer Richardson, giving them a 3-1 win on aggregate.

The bookmakers had had Watford as narrow favourites going into the final on 21 May, but it was a more comfortable win for them than many had expected. The opening goal came in the 25th minute through Jay DeMerit who, after losing his marker at a corner, was able to head the ball into the back of the net from five yards out. Their lead was doubled almost an hour into the match as Neil Sullivan scored an own goal. James Chambers turned and shot after receiving a long throw, the ball was deflected off Eddie Lewis, and it hit the

Leeds post before taking another and decisive deflection off goalkeeper Sullivan. Watford extended their lead in the 84th minute when Spring made a run forward and passed the ball into King. The latter was brought down, and the resulting penalty was converted by Darius Henderson.

Watford's return to the top flight wasn't a happy one. By 20 January 2007 the Hornets had recorded just one win, taking an additional nine points from draws in 22 games. Defeats to Manchester United and Bolton Wanderers were sandwiched between wins over Blackburn Rovers and West Ham United, but the remainder of the season saw them win two, draw four and lose six as they found themselves rooted to the foot of the Premier League table and relegated after just one season.

* * *

Season 2006/07

Championship play-off final

28 May 2007

Derby County 1 (Pearson 61)

West Bromwich Albion 0

When Derby County were relegated from the Premier League in 2002, they were expected to make a bid towards an immediate return. Instead, they struggled all through the 2002/03 season and that had cost John Gregory his job in March. He was replaced by George Burley, with the former Ipswich manager leading them to an 18th-placed finish.

The following season didn't bring any improvement and they ended up 20th in Burley's first full campaign in charge and finished just a point above the relegation zone, with their safety confirmed in the penultimate game against Millwall.

Ahead of the 2004/05 season, Derby didn't have a lot of money to spend. Burley was forced to rely on free transfers and youth talent as he pushed the Rams back towards the Premier League. He had played the market well and brought in the services of Iñigo Idiakez and Grzegorz Rasiak, with the latter netting 17 goals. Their start hadn't been amazing, however; Derby only won four times in their opening 14 games, taking a further four points from draws in that time. They began to pick up results, losing five more times by the time April had arrived while taking 45 points. That had been followed by a run of five games won and three lost.

The play-offs had seen them lose to Preston North End, but Derby had high hopes for the new season. In the summer, the mood had changed. Burley quit as manager in June after a series of disagreements with the club's board, including the sale of youngster

Tom Huddlestone to Tottenham without his knowledge, and Phil Brown was appointed as his replacement. Brown had only been the caretaker at Bolton in 1999, so the Rams had taken a gamble and hoped the new manager could build upon Burley's good work.

He couldn't do that, and their poor form dragged them into a relegation entanglement instead. By January, Brown was sacked following a 3-1 FA Cup defeat at League One side Colchester United and with his team languishing in 19th in the Championship. Academy manager Terry Westley was made caretaker boss but, despite no wins in his first five games, he was given until the end of the season. His first win followed two days later, beating Plymouth 1-0, before he slightly improved Derby's form and had confirmed Championship survival with a few games to spare.

Westley wasn't offered the permanent manager's position, with the job going to Billy

Davies instead. The former Preston man had started to build a side made to compete towards the top of the table but from Derby's start to the 2006/07 season this wasn't apparent. The Rams picked up just five points in their opening six games before recording only their second win of the season, beating Wolves.

The win over the West Midlands side had proved to be the catalyst, propelling Derby towards the play-offs. From that result they picked up 39 points in 18 games and were beaten just three times in that run before going down to their seventh defeat of the season on Boxing Day. They were soon embarking on another good run, winning six of their next seven games, before they ended the campaign with six wins, three draws and three losses. Their third-placed finish saw them face Southampton in the play-offs, while it was a Midlands derby between West Brom and Wolves in the other semi-final.

Southampton were the hosts in their first leg with Derby, and it was they who had the advantage early in the match as Andrew Surman scored with a strike from 20 yards out, but Steve Howard scored either side of half-time for the Rams to secure a 2-1 win. The second leg was just three days later with Derby holding the early advantage at their place as Darren Moore scored after just three minutes. The lead lasted for a minute as Jhon Viáfara netted for the Saints and the half ended level. Viáfara scored again ten minutes into the second half, but Derby replied through an own goal by Leon Best to level the night at 2-2 and restore their aggregate advantage. In the 89th minute, Grzegorz Rasiak scored against his old club to make it 3-2 to Southampton and 4-4 overall, sending the tie into extra time. The extra 30 minutes didn't produce a winner so penalties settled things and Iñigo Idiakez, another former Ram, missed Southampton's fifth penalty to send Derby into the final.

West Brom travelled to Molineux for their first leg and took the lead over their local rivals as Kevin Phillips scored midway through the first half, before Jody Craddock equalised with a header just before half-time. Seyi Olofinjana then put the hosts ahead early in the second half, but Phillips netted his second two minutes later and Diomansy Kamara then made it 3-2 to the Albion in the 73rd minute. The second leg came four days later with the first half remaining goalless. Phillips was on hand to score once again midway through the second half with a header. That was the only goal of the second leg and West Brom progressed with a 4-2 win on aggregate.

The 2007 Championship season marked the return of Wembley hosting the play-off finals. Both West Brom and Derby had been founding members of the Football League in 1888 and had spent the majority of their history competing in the top division, but only one would return there for 2007/08. There was very little to separate the two sides apart from Stephen Pearson's 61st-minute goal. The midfielder got on the end of a pass from Giles Barnes, sliding the ball into the bottom corner and thus taking Derby back to the Premier League. Their promotion was said to be worth up to £60m for the club.

In the summer of 2007, Derby spent £10.5m with the signings of Rob Earnshaw (Norwich City), Tyrone Mears (West Ham United), Andy Todd (Blackburn Rovers), Claude Davis (Sheffield United) and Kenny Miller (Celtic). Despite spending some money to improve the squad, the Rams' season went down as the worst in Premier League history with just 11 points from their 38 games and Derby returned to the Championship.

Their only win of the season came at home to Newcastle United on 17 September, with the additional eight points coming from draws with Portsmouth, Bolton, Fulham (twice), Newcastle, Manchester City, Birmingham and Sunderland.

* * *

I spoke with Ryan Dilks, a Derby supporter and host of the *Second Tier Podcast*, about the club's time in the Championship and Premier League.

Derby were a Premier League team from 1996/97 until their relegation in 2002. Did you ever think they would have got there again?

RD: Definitely. I've always considered Derby to be a massive Championship club, and it always seemed like we would get another chance. It was going to take a rebuild, but we knew we'd have our time again eventually.

Derby finished fourth in 2004/05, after two seasons at the bottom end of the

second tier. What helped change the club's fortunes?

RD: This was more or less down to Derby making two unbelievable signings in Idiakez and Rasiak on free transfers. The club really struggled for money at the time so to bring in two players of that quality was incredibly savvy and having two academy players in Lee Camp and Tom Huddlestone be given their chances in the first team also massively helped as the pair were revelations.

The 2004/05 season saw Derby fall short in the semi-finals, and they didn't get another play-off opportunity until 2006/07. Was it only a matter of time before the team got it right and how confident were you the second time around?

RD: It was looking pretty bleak at the time. Derby were in a right mess financially and it almost felt like if we didn't get promoted, then it was going to be a long way back. Fortunately, Peter Gadsby saved the club and put us on the right path.

I wasn't hugely confident [going into the 2007 play-offs], and it felt like we had blown our chance of promotion after missing out on the top two. Southampton, West Brom and Wolves all had strong sides while it felt like we were overachieving with what we had. Billy Davies did a fantastic job getting us to this point, so we had belief that anything was possible.

After scrapping through on penalties against Southampton, Derby faced West Brom in the final. How were you feeling about the final?

RD: I wasn't very confident. We still felt like underdogs despite finishing above West Brom. They had such an experienced side, so it felt like the only way we were going to win was by making it a cagey game and taking our chances when they came.

It was sheer jubilation when we sealed victory. It's a feeling you don't get to feel as much as a Derby fan and the Premier League had taken significant strides since we were last in it. It felt like the Hollywood of football, so the inclusion of Derby felt obscene.

The season that followed for Derby has gone down as the worst in Premier League history and the lowest-ever points total. Did you expect to go straight back to the Championship?

RD: We were very aware that we would be up against it. We had the smallest budget in the division and were promoted with a squad that felt like it overachieved at Championship level, let alone in the Premier League.

I don't think many expected us to get panned as much as we did, though, and, in the end, every signing we made went disastrously.

People may be surprised to read this, but I actually enjoyed that season. After numerous 5-0 losses, the pain doesn't really affect you any more, so while it was an embarrassing season in many ways, it's one I do look back on with fondness.

With Derby currently fighting towards the bottom of the Championship, do you ever see a day when the club might be back in the Premier League?

RD: It'll be a long way back. Of course, we came close on many occasions in the 2010s. With the current divide between the Premier League and Championship, clubs like Derby have a lot of work to do just to get to the dance. A club this size will hopefully always be destined for a spot in the top flight again eventually, but right now it feels a long way off.

* * *

Season 2007/08

Championship play-off final

24 May 2008

Bristol City 0

Hull City 1 (Windass 38)

The play-off final at the end of the 2007/08 season had offered a new opportunity for both Hull City and Bristol City. While it had been 28 years since the Robins had last featured in the top tier of English football, Hull had never set foot at such heights.

Hull had been in the Championship since their promotion from League One in 2004/05 and it had been their second consecutive promotion after finishing second in the Third Division the previous season. The 2004/05 season had begun with just one loss in five games, with a defeat to Port Vale being sandwiched in between two wins. The east

Yorkshire side didn't set the world alight for the next 11 games, but they did collect 20 points from the 33 available, with a defeat to Swindon Town being preceded by a nine-game unbeaten stretch, taking 25 points before a loss to Doncaster ended that. A slight drop in form was followed by a run of six wins and two draws before ending the campaign with two wins, two draws and four losses. Despite the nervy end to the season, the Tigers finished second.

Life in the Championship under the management of Peter Taylor hadn't got off to a flying start as they finished 18th in 2005/06. A third of their victories that season had come by 2 October, but that run also saw them draw six and lose five. The Tigers continued to struggle for form as they took just two points in the next six games. As they approached the second half of the season, they continued to have mixed form. A run of five wins, three draws and eight defeats had taken them through from early December to early March before they ended the season with 14 points in nine games, losing just once in that run. It hadn't been the best campaign, but Hull had avoided straight relegation back to the third tier.

Before the 2006/07 season had started, there was a change of manager after Taylor left to take up the job vacated by Iain Dowie at Crystal Palace. Phil Parkinson was confirmed as his replacement in late June. The new boss didn't waste time in using the £1m they had received from Palace for defender Leon Cort in readiness for the new season, but 2006/07 was marginally worse than the previous year, resulting in Hull finishing 21st and just seven points above the relegation zone.

With the Tigers in the relegation zone, Parkinson was sacked after their 4-2 defeat at home to Southampton on 2 December, with his assistant Phil Brown taking over until the end of the season. Brown kept Hull afloat in the Championship and continued in his role into 2007/08 as the Tigers looked to pursue their dream of reaching the top flight. There was no real consistency in their opening 14 games of the season as they won just four while drawing four and losing six, but their form picked up. Their best run came midway through March and well into April with 16 points from 18 available, the season ending with losses to Sheffield United and Ipswich Town either side of a win over Crystal Palace. Brown's men finished third in the table, seeing them feature in the play-offs alongside Bristol City, Crystal Palace and Watford.

Hull's first leg against Watford was at Vicarage Road on 11 May. Nick Barmby gave the Tigers an early lead, scoring after just eight minutes, before Dean Windass added a second in the 27th minute. That advantage was taken into the second leg three days later, with a nice lead turning into an empathic win in Hull. Darius Henderson had pulled one back in the tie for Watford, netting in the 12th minute, before Barmby restored the two-goal cushion just before half-time. Caleb Folan added their second of the night in the 70th minute before Richard Garcia and Nathan Doyle scored in the 88th and 90th minutes respectively to seal their place in the final.

Down in south London, Bristol City had taken the lead twice to secure a 2-1 win over Crystal Palace. The first leg at Selhurst Park on 10 May had had a goalless first half before Louis Carey netted the opening goal in the 53rd minute. It had looked like it was going to be the winner until Ben Watson smashed home a penalty in the 87th minute, conceded by Carey. It was a temporary reprieve for Palace, though, as David Noble struck an effort from 30 yards out in injury time to seal the victory for the Robins. City welcomed the Eagles to the south-west three days later, hoping to seal their place in the final at home. Palace's plan to spoil the party was in full swing as Watson netted midway through the first half to level the tie on aggregate. That was the only goal of the 90 minutes, meaning the teams required extra time to settle it.

Lee Trundle scored City's first goal of the evening, putting the ball in the back of the net towards the end of the first period, before Michael McIndoe added a second after the break, putting Bristol City 4-2 ahead on aggregate. The referee's final blast of his whistle confirmed the Robins' participation in the final against Hull.

The Wembley showdown on 24 May was cagey and despite being dominant in the opening minutes, Bristol City found themselves 1-0 down just before half-time as Dean Windass volleyed the ball past Adriano Basso from the edge of the box after Fraizer Campbell delivered a pinpoint ball to the forward. The Robins went closest towards the end of the match when a weak punch from Boaz Myhill allowed Trundle the opportunity to equalise, but his effort was blocked before substitute Darren Byfield went close twice: his first effort was a header just over the bar followed by a shot fired wide of the post. Hull saw it through to win promotion to the top flight for the first time in their history.

The Tigers lasted two seasons in the Premier League. In 2008/09 they finished 17th before they were relegated in 2010, finishing 19th. Their start to 2008/09 hadn't been one expected from a side facing relegation. Hull lost one game by 25 October, taking 20 points from their opening nine games, before their downfall saw them win just twice more and collect an additional nine points with draws. The following season wasn't too dissimilar;

Charlton Athletic celebrate their First Division play-off victory over Sunderland at Wembley Stadium in May 1998

Alan Curbishley lifts the trophy above his head after securing promotion to the Premier League

Bolton Wanderers manager Sam Allardyce holds up the trophy after securing promotion to the top flight

Jubilant Ipswich Town celebrate promotion at Wembley following their 4-2 win over Barnsley

Crystal Palace captain Neil Shipperley runs in celebration of his goal against West Ham United in Cardiff, 2004

Bobby Zamora celebrates with team-mates in front of West Ham supporters after scoring the winning goal against Preston North End

West Ham United celebrate their promotion to the Premier League after beating Preston 1-0 in the play-off final

Dean Windass scores Hull City's goal in their match with Bristol City at Wembley in May 2008

A nervous Hull fan looks on during the Tigers match with Bristol City at Wembley circa 2008

Steven Caldwell lifts the Championship play-off trophy after victory against Sheffield United alongside his Burnley team-mates

Scott Sinclair celebrates his hat-trick for Swansea City against Reading in May 2011

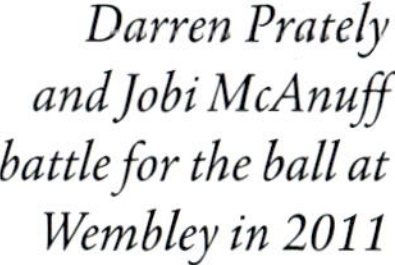

Darren Prately and Jobi McAnuff battle for the ball at Wembley in 2011

Norwich City fans celebrate during their Championship play-off final against Middlesbrough

David Wagner and Jaap Stam pace on the touchline during their sides' close battle at Wembley in 2017

Nottingham Forest fans sing ahead of their play-off final with Huddersfield Town at Wembley in 2022

Nottingham Forest celebrate their play-off victory with the trophy

Luton Town players run in celebration of their penalty shoot-out win over Coventry City at Wembley in May 2023

Jack Stephens lifts the Championship play-off trophy in a shower of champagne as Southampton celebrate victory over Leeds United

Russell Martin embraces opposition manager Daniel Farke following Southampton's shoot-out win over Leeds United at Wembley

Connor Roberts dejected amongst team-mates after Leeds United were defeated at Wembley by Southampton in May 2024

eight points in 11 games had been followed by a run of two wins and two draws before the remainder of the season saw just another 14 points collected. The haul of 30 points saw them relegated back to the Championship.

* * *

Season 2008/09

Championship play-off final

25 May 2009

Burnley 1 (Elliott 13)

Sheffield United 0

Burnley had finished in the top half of the Championship just twice before they finished fifth in the 2008/09 season. After promotion from what was then the Second Division in 2000, they narrowly missed out on back-to-back play-off appearances as they finished seventh in both 2000/01 and 2001/02. The seasons that followed had seen them record six bottom-half finishes: 16th, 19th, 13th, 17th, 15th and 13th again, between 2002 and 2008.

With Burnley not being in the top flight for 33 years, the expectation on them to achieve it in 2008/09 certainly wasn't there. August might have given Owen Coyle's men an idea of how it might've gone: two points from their four games in the opening month had left them sitting 23rd in the table. From their first win, at Nottingham Forest on 13 September, they kicked on and slowly climbed up the table towards the play-offs. Apart from a run of five consecutive losses in December and January, Burnley enjoyed largely good form and found themselves fifth after beating Bristol City 4-0 on the final day.

Burnley faced Reading in the semi-final after the Royals had finished a point ahead of them. Reading dominated the first leg, but it wasn't decided until late in the second half when Graham Alexander scored for Burnley from the penalty spot. The second leg three days later saw another goalless first half before a 51st-minute strike by Martin Paterson put Burnley ahead on the night. Seven minutes later, Thompson doubled the lead with a looping volley and the Clarets won 3-0 on aggregate.

Sheffield United met Preston at Deepdale in the first leg of their semi-final. The home side had taken the lead in the first half when Sean St Ledger scored, but the tie was level soon into the second half with a volley from Brian Howard 21 seconds after kick-off. The return leg at Bramall Lane was decided by a single goal: Greg Halford's 59th-minute header secured a 1-0 win for United on the night and a 2-1 victory on aggregate.

Coyle had Burnley playing with freedom and ambition as the founding members of the Football League sought a place in the Premier League. The biggest stage in English football arguably required a strike worthy to be a Wembley winner and that's what Clarets fans got: Wade Elliott hit a sensational curling effort in the 13th minute, nestling into the top corner. Chances came and went for both sides, but the match finished 1-0, confirming Burnley's promotion.

In the summer of 2009, Burnley spent £3.85m bringing in Steven Fletcher from Hibernian, Tyrone Mears from Derby and Brian Easton from Hamilton Academical, but the new additions weren't able to help Burnley survive longer than a season in the top flight. After winning five of their opening 11 games, the Clarets picked up just 15 more points between November and May. Owen Coyle remained in charge until early January with the team sitting 14th, but his replacement, Brian Laws, was not able to change their ever-likely relegation as the Lancashire club continued their fall to the bottom three.

* * *

Season 2009/10

Championship play-off final

22 May 2010

Blackpool 3 (Adam 13; Taylor-Fletcher 41; Ormerod 45+1)

Cardiff City 2 (Chopra 9; Ledley 37)

Promotion from League One via the play-offs at the end of the 2006/07 season hadn't brought Blackpool instant success in the Championship. Simon Grayson had helped the side finish third in the third tier before going on to beat Oldham Athletic and Yeovil Town in the play-offs to join Scunthorpe United and Bristol City in the second tier.

Their first two years in the Championship had seen them finish 19th and 16th. The 2008/09 season, in which they finished slightly higher than the previous year, had seen them struggle for consistent form and bounce between mid-table and the relegation zone. Grayson's final game in charge had come by way of a 1-1 home draw with Swansea on 20 December 2008 before he departed to take over at Leeds. His assistant Tony Parkes replaced him and after a run that saw them take just ten points from 12 games, Parkes led them to 16th after losing just one in the final ten games.

It was no surprise that Parkes didn't get the job permanently, with the club owners, the Oyston family, appointing an experienced manager in Ian Holloway. Under Holloway, Blackpool began to pull together better runs of results. They opened the season with just one defeat in the opening nine games, taking 16 points. Back-to-back away defeats had been followed by another decent run, taking 11 points from five games before their form took a hit. From late November they won six, drew five and lost ten before they ended the campaign with just one loss in the final nine: six wins, two draws and a heavy defeat to champions Newcastle United led them to a sixth-placed finish. They had almost missed out on the play-offs altogether as Swansea required just three points in their final home game on the last day of the season to pip them to the final spot. The Swans were held to a 0-0 draw by Doncaster Rovers, thus keeping Blackpool in the promotion hunt.

Blackpool faced Nottingham Forest in the semi-finals, with the first leg at Bloomfield Road finishing 2-1 in their favour. They conceded in the 13th minute through Chris Cohen before coming from behind to take the advantage, the goals coming from Keith Southern and a penalty for Charlie Adams. When the sides met again at the City Ground, Blackpool twice fell behind. An equaliser came through DJ Campbell after Robert Earnshaw had scored an early goal before Stephen Dobbie brought the game back level after Earnshaw netted his second. Blackpool then took the lead with two quick-fire goals: Campbell scoring twice to complete his hat-trick in the 76th and 79th minutes respectively. Forest striker Dele Adebola scored a late consolation goal in injury time, but Blackpool advanced to the final, winning 6-4 on aggregate.

Fourth-placed Cardiff City faced Leicester City in the other semi-final. The first leg had been decided by a single goal from Cardiff's Peter Whittingham, who scored a free kick in the 78th minute, then the second leg got off to the perfect start for the Bluebirds when Michael Chopra doubled the Bluebirds' aggregate lead. An equaliser from Matty Fryatt on the night and an own goal from Mark Hudson then made it 2-2 on aggregate. Then Andy King gave Leicester the overall advantage with a goal just after half-time before the tie was level again when Cardiff were awarded a penalty with just over 20 minutes to play, with Whittingham scoring it. The game went to extra time, but no further goals were scored, and a penalty shoot-out was needed.

Both sides scored each of their first three kicks, before David Marshall saved a panenka attempt from Leicester's Yann Kermorgant. Mark Kennedy gave Cardiff the lead and Marshall then saved another one with Martyn Waghorn's miss seeing the Welsh club progress.

The three previous play-off finals had finished 1-0, but the 82,244 supporters who attended on 22 May were treated to a first-half goal-fest. The opening goal came in the ninth minute when Whittingham played in Chopra, allowing the striker to score past Matt Gilks into the bottom corner. The lead lasted for just four minutes, however, after Charlie Adam hit a free kick around the wall and into the net. The Bluebirds regrouped after Blackpool had gained control in the game and retook the lead in the 37th minute: Whittingham turned provider once again as he got the ball to Joe Ledley with the latter scoring. Blackpool equalised four minutes later when a corner was fumbled by goalkeeper Marshall with the ball falling to Gary Taylor-Fletcher, who turned it into the back of the net. Then they continued to press and took the lead in injury time when a deflected shot off Brett Ormerod gave Blackpool a 3-2 lead. All the goals had been exhausting in the first half and the scoreline remained the same in the second half, seeing Blackpool earn their Premier League place.

The talk in the lead-up to the new season had been centred around the lack of activity from the club's hierarchy with 81 days passing between the play-off final and their first arrivals at Bloomfield Road. Ian Holloway had just 15 players at his disposal but, by 11 August, the departed players had been replaced. The first half of the season didn't go badly for Blackpool; after taking seven points from their opening four games and despite a 6-0 hammering by Arsenal, the Tangerines sat fourth in the table. They won an additional five times before the new year while drawing three more and losing five. They remained in the top half by the end of December, but the second half of the season saw their form unravel.

Back-to-back losses to Manchester City and Birmingham were their first two of 13 defeats. They also only won three more times in 2011 and took a haul of five points from draws. A run of three defeats to Fulham, Arsenal and Wigan Athletic pushed them into the relegation zone, and although three draws on the bounce briefly lifted them to 17th, a defeat at Manchester United on the final day relegated them back to the Championship.

The 2010s

Season 2010/11

Championship play-off final

30 May 2011

Reading 2 (Allen 49 og; Mills 57)

Swansea City 4 (Sinclair 21 pen, 22, 80 pen; Dobbie 40)

ROBERTO MARTÍNEZ'S first full season in charge of Swansea City couldn't have gone any better: the Swans finished 2007/08 as Champions of League One, beating Nottingham Forest to the title by ten points.

They had flirted with the top six for a third of the campaign before an impressive run of wins lifted them into top spot, a position they didn't yield to anyone for the remainder of the season.

Ahead of 2008/09, there wasn't a lot of money to be spent. The club had sold Darryl Duffy to Bristol Rovers for £100,000 in July, but had spent £580,000 on Ashley Williams from Stockport County, as well as signing Gorka Pintado from Granada and Albert Serrán from another Spanish side, Espanyol.

Though they clearly didn't have the biggest budget in the Championship, Swansea found themselves competing towards the top half of the table. By 21 November they had won seven, drawn six and lost five before they found some form with just one loss in 19 games, taking 31 points in that time. They suffered another two defeats and took 11 points from five games before losing their final two. Despite impressive form during the season, Swansea had finished eighth, outside the play-offs by six points and just below their south Wales rivals.

The following season had seen the sale of Jason Scotland for £2m to Wigan Athletic as well as Owain Tudur Jones for £250,000 to Norwich City, with the Swans bringing in Nathan Dyer and Craig Beattie as replacements, for £400,000 and £800,000 from Southampton and West Bromwich Albion respectively. Swansea had also seen the departure of manager Martínez, who joined Wigan. The vacancy was filled by Paulo Sousa.

The season had started with two losses, with Swansea sitting in the relegation zone after those games, but things soon improved. They followed that with just one defeat in 15 games, taking 28 points from that run and climbing all the way to fourth. A reverse to Newcastle United and a draw with Peterborough United had briefly dropped them out of the play-offs, but after returning to winning ways against Plymouth Argyle in December, they remained in the play-off spots for most of the season, bouncing between fourth and sixth. That was until the final two games. On 17 April, Swansea had beaten Barnsley 3-1 and sat sixth in the table, but then they lost away to Sheffield United and drew with Doncaster Rovers, allowing eventual play-off winners Blackpool to pip them to the final spot.

Another managerial change came ahead of the 2010/11 season: Sousa had left the club by mutual consent, with Brendan Rodgers appointed on a 12-month rolling contract. Their most notable signing had been Scott Sinclair who had signed from Chelsea for £500,000 and it wasn't long before he was making an impact. Swansea sat outside the play-offs for just seven weeks of the season, eventually finishing third with a record of 24 wins, eight draws and 14 defeats. Their position in the table meant they were paired with Nottingham Forest and Cardiff faced Reading.

Swansea travelled to the City Ground in the first leg, but were dealt a blow early in the game as defender Neil Taylor was dismissed for a foul on Lewis McGugan. Despite being down to ten men for 88 minutes, Swansea held on for a 0-0 draw. The return leg came four days later at the Liberty Stadium where Leon Britton put Swansea in the lead with a 25-yard strike before Stephen Dobbie doubled it five minutes later. Rob Earnshaw struck back for Forest in the 78th minute, but a late third goal from Darren Pratley sealed the Swans' passage to the final.

At the Madejski Stadium, Cardiff didn't fare any better than their Welsh counterparts. A goalless draw away to Reading was all they could manage in a game of very few chances before they welcomed the Royals to the Cardiff City Stadium four days later. Reading took the lead in the second leg with Shane Long chipping Stephen Bywater midway through the first half. Long doubled the advantage with his second of the game, netting a penalty on half-time, before Jobi McAnuff scored a third to secure a 3-0 win and their spot at Wembley.

Swansea had beaten Reading home and away during the season, 1-0 each time, but the final produced a far more open game. The first goal came from the penalty spot after a challenge on Nathan Dyer in the box was deemed a foul with Scott Sinclair stepping up and slotting it home. Immediately after the restart, Swansea were back on the attack and Sinclair had quickly doubled his tally a minute later. The dominance continued for the Swans as Dobbie got in on the act, side-footing a Dyer cross beyond goalkeeper Adam Federici five minutes before half-time. Reading pulled one back early in the second half when Noel Hunt's header at the near post from a McAnuff cross was headed into his own net by Joe Allen. The deficit was further reduced in the 57th minute when Matt Mills scored from another McAnuff corner. With the game in the balance, Swansea extended their lead with ten minutes remaining. Fabio Borini was brought down in the box by Andy Griffin with Sinclair stepping up once again, completing his hat-trick in the process, only the second in play-off final history following Clive Mendonca's treble in the 1998 final. It was enough to see Swansea promoted with a 4-2 win.

Swansea spent seven seasons in the Premier League and finished in mid-table in six of them before they were relegated in 2017/18 after finishing 18th. Coming 11th place in 2011/12 had given Swansea supporters a good idea of what to expect from life in the Premier League and the next five seasons saw them finish ninth, 12th, eighth, 12th again and

15th, also winning the League Cup in 2013, before their horrid season in 2017/18. The Swans started with nine points from their opening 15 games before they recorded just their third win on 9 December, beating West Bromwich Albion.

Swansea's horrid results continued as they took four points in the next six games but that was followed by a surprisingly good run of form as they took 15 points from eight matches. In that sequence they lost just once but the last eight games were the complete opposite with just two points won from two draws.

* * *

Season 2011/12

Championship play-off final

19 May 2012

Blackpool 1 (Ince 48)

West Ham United 2 (Cole 35; Vaz Tê 87)

Avram Grant was sacked as West Ham United manager following their relegation from the Premier League at the end of the 2010/11 season. His successor was Sam Allardyce, and his mission was clear: secure promotion.

After losing their opening game of 2011/12, 1-0 to Cardiff City, the Hammers only sat outside the top six for three weeks. That was at the start of the campaign and from week five onwards they didn't look back. For most of the season, West Ham looked on course for automatic promotion, rising to second after their 4-0 win over Blackpool and remaining in contention for the top two until 17 March when they drew with Leeds United. They had also topped the division for a brief period, but they eventually finished third. Failure to win a league game in March had seen the Hammers overtaken by

Reading, who had also beaten them in a key game at Upton Park, and Southampton, despite beating Hull City on the final day.

Allardyce had created the best defensive team, also recording the fewest defeats, but they still had a threat on the attack with the second-best goal difference and only Southampton netting more goals, but too many draws had seen them miss out on one of the automatic spots. Instead, a third-placed finish saw them face Cardiff in the play-off semi-final and compete for a place in the final to face either Birmingham City or Blackpool.

West Ham travelled to Wales for the first leg and came away with a 2-0 win after a Jack Collison brace before the return in London. When the sides met again, goals from Kevin Nolan, Ricardo Vaz Tê and Nicky Maynard secured a 3-0 victory – 5-0 on aggregate – and West Ham's first appearance at Wembley since the 1981 League Cup Final.

Tom Ince's goal at Bloomfield Road had been enough to win Blackpool's opening leg; his long-range shot ricocheted off Birmingham defender Curtis Davies and past Colin Doyle late in the first half. In the return leg five days later, Stephen Dobbie extended Blackpool's aggregate lead on the stroke of half-time. Matt Phillips scored just after the break to make it 3-0 overall before Birmingham's Nikola Žigić scored midway through the second half. Davies reduced Blackpool's advantage to a single goal, but it wasn't enough for a comeback as the tie finished 3-2 on aggregate.

In front of the Wembley crowd on 19 May, chances had come and gone for both sides, and the deadlock was broken in the 35th minute. Matt Taylor made a cross-field pass to Carlton Cole with the forward taking one touch before shooting the ball beyond Matt Gilks. The lead lasted until just after half-time as Blackpool levelled three minutes after the restart: a Matt Phillips pass fell to Ince whose first-time strike beat Rob Green in the West Ham goal. The score remained level until the 87th minute when the Londoners reestablished their lead, Vaz Tê picking up a loose ball and firing it into the roof of the Blackpool net, with no further goals scored. West Ham's immediate return to the Premier League was complete.

The Hammers have remained in the Premier League since their promotion in 2012 with their return to the top flight ending in a tenth-placed finish. Since then they've achieved finishes ranging from a high of sixth in 2020/21 and a low of 16th the following season, also winning the UEFA Conference League in 2022/23. As of the spring of 2025, West Ham sat in the bottom third of the Premier League table, albeit with what looked to be a big-enough gap between themselves and the relegation zone.

* * *

Season 2012/13

Championship play-off final

27 May 2013

Crystal Palace 1 (Phillips 105 pen)

Watford 0

(After extra time)

After finishing sixth at the end of the 2005/06 season and losing to Watford in the play-off semi-final, and losing to Bristol City at the same stage two years later, there had been little danger of Crystal Palace pursuing promotion back to the Premier League.

From 2008/09 the Eagles had finished 15th, 21st, 20th and 17th, far away from the top six. That changed in 2012/13 when a major improvement saw Palace back towards the top end of the table. There hadn't been a great deal of money spent in the summer either. Joel Ward had signed from Portsmouth for around £400,000, while the transfers of Yannick Bolasie from Bristol City and Darcy Blake from Cardiff City were for undisclosed fees (though they were all within the same price bracket).

If the start to the campaign had been anything to go by, no one would have even included Crystal Palace in their top-ten predictions, never mind the play-offs. Losses to Watford, Bristol City and Middlesbrough had left them rock bottom of the Championship table, but things quickly changed and a win over Sheffield Wednesday on 1 September sparked a 14-game unbeaten run. By the end of the run, Crystal Palace sat at the summit of the table, but they dropped into second with a defeat to Leeds United. Another unbeaten run of seven points in five games had been followed by mixed form as the Eagles won seven, drew eight and lost seven, but the drop-off wasn't terminal as Palace sat in the play-offs by the end of the season. The rest of the play-off spots had been occupied by Watford, Brighton & Hove Albion and Leicester City with Crystal Palace facing Brighton for a spot in the Wembley final.

The first leg at Selhurst Park finished goalless before the sides faced off again three days later on the South Coast. The venue for the second leg, Brighton's new Amex Stadium, had been a haven for the Seagulls who hadn't lost a game there since January. Despite this, Wilfried Zaha put Palace ahead midway through the second half after an assist from Yannick Bolasie before the scorer doubled their advantage late on, and that was enough to qualify for the final.

Watford travelled to the East Midlands to face Leicester in the first leg, but left on the back of a 1-0 defeat; David Nugent's header from an

Anthony Knockaert free kick late on was the difference going into the return. Matěj Vydra put Watford ahead at Vicarage Road with a left-footed volley from a Marco Cassetti pass into the far corner of Kasper Schmeichel's goal. Nugent restored parity with another header from a Knockaert corner before Vydra scored his second and levelled the semi-final 2-2 on aggregate. The moment that followed remains in football legend: Leicester were awarded an injury-time penalty with Knockaert stepping up to take it. The spot kick was saved, and in the immediate counterattack Jonathan Hogg's knock-down at the other end was finished by Troy Deeney to make it 3-2 and send the Hornets to Wembley.

After 90 minutes of the final neither side could find the breakthrough and the game went to extra time. The only goal arrived right on the brink of half-time with Zaha fouled by Cassetti in the Watford box and the penalty was struck into the top corner by Phillips, putting Palace ahead. Despite several chances for Watford, they came to nothing, and Crystal Palace were promoted to the Premier League.

Following their promotion to the Premier League, Crystal Palace have been in no danger of returning to the second tier. After an 11th-placed finish in 2013/14, the Eagles have gone on to end up tenth, 15th, 14th, 11th, 12th, 14th another two times, 12th, 11th and tenth, and were firmly in mid-table by the time of going to print.

***

Season 2013/14

Championship play-off final

24 May 2014

Derby County 0

Queens Park Rangers 1 (Zamora 90)

The surprise introduction of telecom giant BT to the world of Premier League football had meant the money being pumped into the prize fund almost doubled from £1.7bn to just over £3bn ahead of the 2013/14 season.

Queens Park Rangers had spent two seasons in the Premier League after they were promoted from the Championship as champions in 2010/11, but after finishes of 17th and 20th they were relegated in 2013. Their last promotion to the Premier League had come at the end of a campaign that had seen them spend all but two weeks at the summit of the Championship, where they ended with 88 points.

Neil Warnock had led his side on an impressive run to begin the 2010/11 season. The Hoops had taken 49 points from their opening 19 games, winning 11 and drawing eight, before they fell to their first two defeats in December. They briefly returned to winning ways at the end of the year, but they were introduced to the new year with a defeat. Their good form soon returned with an 11-game unbeaten run taking them from January through to March with a defeat to London rivals Millwall ending that. There was no need to panic, though. Three wins got their promotion push back on track and although they ended the season with two defeats, promotion was comfortable.

Their return to the Premier League had been far from outstanding, however. Warnock had overseen 20 games before his dismissal, with the club sitting 17th and with only 17 points on the board. His replacement, Mark Hughes, lost his first game before winning his first points with a victory and draw over Wigan and Aston Villa respectively. The rest of February and early March had seen the dismal form continue as QPR took a single point across five games, seeing out the season with five wins and five losses.

Relegation had been avoided by the skin of their teeth, surviving over Bolton by a single point. After just keeping the club up, Hughes was given the chance to change their fortunes and continued as manager into the 2012/13 season, but after taking just four points in their opening 12 games he was replaced by Harry Redknapp towards the end of November.

Redknapp's first game in charge ended in defeat to Manchester United at Old Trafford. He won his first point in a goalless draw with Sunderland, before taking a further five points in the three games that followed. A poor end to the previous year and an unbeaten start to 2013 had seen them take seven points in the five games between January and February before they ended the season with just two more wins, collecting a total of eight points in the final 13 games. Their 25 points left them rock bottom of the Premier League and 12 points from safety. Despite this, Redknapp had shown enough to continue as manager as QPR sought immediate return from the Championship in 2013/14.

When the new season had swung round, QPR were excited for what was to come, and they had every right to feel that way as it would never see QPR sit below the play-off positions. The season began with an impressive 11-game unbeaten run consisting of eight wins and three draws before their first defeat came at the hands of Burnley. They had another unbeaten run shortly after, but a defeat to Doncaster Rovers had swiftly ended that run before it had a chance to build.

They lost just twice in a run of 11 games between December and February before their form for the remainder of the season was mixed. After three consecutive losses in February, the Hoops were beaten a further five times, while winning seven and drawing three. They dropped from second to fourth so missed out on automatic promotion, but they still had a chance through the play-offs. Leicester City and Burnley finished in the top two while Queens Park Rangers joined Derby County, Wigan Athletic and Brighton in the play-offs with the London side facing Wigan in the semi-final.

Harry Redknapp's side travelled to the DW Stadium for their first leg, but it was far from an entertaining game; there were very few chances in the goalless draw. The second leg was three days later at Loftus Road, but despite having home advantage, QPR conceded the first goal, through James Perch but, the tie was level once again when Charlie Austin equalised from the penalty spot in the 73rd minute. It finished 1-1 after 90 minutes with extra time needed to settle the tie: Austin netted again in the 96th minute, beating Scott Carson with his effort, to send QPR into the final.

Brighton welcomed Derby to the South Coast in their first leg and took the lead in the 18th minute through Jesse Lingard. The equaliser followed with Chris Martin making no mistake from the penalty spot after Matthew Upson fouled Craig Forsyth, before a third goal was scored in the first half to give the Rams the advantage going into the second leg. It was a strange goal as Martin's shot rebounded off the bar, striking keeper Tomasz Kuszczak on the back and crossing the line for an own goal, but Derby didn't care as it proved the winner. That lead was extended in the second leg when Will Hughes scored from a Jamie Ward cross before Chris Martin doubled the advantage on the day in the second half. The Rams later added a third to make it 5-1 on aggregate through George Thorne's volley, and Jeff Hendrick scored from a Patrick Bamford pass, before Brighton got a consolation goal through Kazenga LuaLua as it finished 6-2 on aggregate.

There were no goals in the first half in the final, but the game wasn't without its chances. The best opportunities were from corners and free kicks, but neither side could make their set pieces count. QPR's afternoon was made tougher when Gary O'Neil was dismissed on the hour mark for a professional foul on Johnny Russell, but their hopes of promotion weren't over. Substitute Bobby Zamora had come on and done his job as he netted the only goal of the contest with a curling effort past Lee Grant in the 90th minute, sealing the west Londoners' return to the Premier League.

Rangers' stay in the top flight was brief as they were relegated straight back to the Championship in 2014/15. They spent all but ten of their matchdays in the relegation zone and started the season with back-to-back defeats, against Hull and Tottenham. Their first taste of victory came at home to Sunderland but they followed that up with one point in five games. Aston Villa were beaten in October, but the win remained isolated as QPR began November with a defeat away to Chelsea before they took 12 points from ten games after winning three, drawing three and losing four.

That was their best form of the season with the next ten games between January and late March seeing the team win one and lose the nine others as they hovered above the drop zone. QPR had dropped back into the relegation zone shortly after and had finished the season with eight points in as many games. Their haul of 30 points saw them finish rock bottom of the division, eight points off Sunderland and Aston Villa, who had both survived relegation ahead of Hull, Burnley and the Hoops.

* * *

Season 2014/15

Championship play-off final

25 May 2015

Middlesbrough 0

Norwich City 2 (Jerome 12; Redmond 15)

Expectations for Norwich City were high ahead of the 2013/14 season after the club had achieved an 11th-place finish in the Premier League the previous year. The expectations got higher following the summer transfer window in which Norwich had spent a record amount. Ricky van Wolfswinkel was signed for a club-record fee of £8.5m while Gary Hooper, Leroy Fer, Carlo Nash, Martin Olsson and Nathan Redmond all joined on permanent deals.

The season started with four points in the opening three games before a further four losses and another four points left Norwich in a poor position. November saw a heavy 7-0 defeat to Manchester City, but their form did show some signs of improvement. From November through to late March, the Canaries won six, drew six and lost 11 before they finished the season with just a single point in six games. Their failure to win in those final few weeks cost them their Premier League status as they finished 18th and three points behind West Bromwich Albion, returning to the Championship after three seasons.

Before a ball was kicked in 2014/15, Norwich were considered one of the favourites for promotion. On top of signing Conor McGrandles from Falkirk for around £1m, the Canaries had also brought in Lewis Grabban (Bournemouth), Kyle Lafferty (Palermo), Gary O'Neil (Queens Park Rangers), Carlos Cuéllar (Sunderland) and Cameron Jerome (Stoke City). The incomings had been to replace some big players departing the club:

Robert Snodgrass was signed by Hull City for £7m while Anthony Pilkington and Leroy Fer departed for Cardiff City and Queens Park Rangers for £1m and £8m respectively.

A loss on the opening day at Wolverhampton Wanderers was followed by a good run of six wins and two draws before they were beaten again at the end of September. Their form took a hit shortly after as they won just once in a stretch of nine games but that was behind them by December, losing only four more times while taking 59 points between December and the end of the season. This impressive sequence catapulted them into third place and comfortably into the play-offs alongside Middlesbrough, Brentford and Ipswich Town.

Norwich hadn't actually been far off the automatic promotion spots. They finished four points behind champions Bournemouth and three points below runners-up Watford, but after just missing out they travelled to their

East Anglian rivals Ipswich for the first leg of their play-off semi-final. Jonny Howson put Norwich into the lead, but Ipswich were level by the break with Paul Anderson scoring. The match ended level and the second leg at Carrow Road saw the sides remain level after 45 minutes of play. The deadlock was broken just after half-time as Ipswich conceded a penalty: defender Christophe Berra had deliberately blocked Nathan Redmond's shot with his hand, resulting in a chance for Norwich and the culprit facing his marching orders with a red card. Wes Hoolahan's successful spot kick fired the Canaries into the lead, but Tommy Smith ensured a level game once again with a goal on the hour. Further goals from Redmond and Cameron Jerome ensured a 3-1 win for Norwich and progression to the final with a 4-2 aggregate success.

Middlesbrough and Brentford met for the right to reach Wembley with the latter hosting the first leg. Jelle Vossen gave Boro the lead in the first half with a header from an Andy Clayton cross before Andre Gray equalised 11 minutes into the second half. The hosts dominated the second half, but the winner came from the Teesside club deep into injury time through Fernando Amorebieta. Even in the second leg at the Riverside, Brentford dominated, but goals from Lee Tomlin, Kike and Albert Adomah saw Middlesbrough win 3-0 on the night and 5-1 on aggregate.

It had been reported that the final was worth around £120m to the winning club over a three-year period through sponsorship and television deals, and Norwich were considered narrow favourites to seal victory against Boro. The game was decided in a brief three-minute period in the first half: in the 12th minute, Cameron Jerome opened the scoring after taking the ball into the box and enticing the goalkeeper to come out before beating him at the near post, then Redmond doubled the lead three minutes later as he ran on to a pass from Steven Whittaker. With those two goals, Norwich were promoted to the Premier League.

Just two losses in the opening seven games of the season saw Norwich make a decent start on their return to the top flight, sitting mid-table with nine points. Their form dropped following a defeat to Leicester City and they took eight points in the next 11 games before they ended 2015 and started 2016 with wins against Aston Villa and Southampton. Despite those back-to-back victories, Norwich saw their horrid form continue: two points in ten games between January and March were followed by more successive wins, before they ended the season three points in the final six games. Nine wins and seven draws wasn't enough to keep them in the top flight as they finished 18th.

* * *

Season 2015/16

Championship play-off final

28 May 2016

Hull City 1 (Diamé 71)

Sheffield Wednesday 0

The Tigers had barely flirted with the bottom of the Premier League table before they were relegated in 2014/15, having won promotion two years earlier. Two defeats in their opening three games of 2014/14 had left them sitting 17th, just above the relegation zone, before they pulled themselves towards mid-table. Eight points in four games had steered them away from potential danger before the first half of the season saw them win an additional three while drawing three more and losing a further six. A hefty 6-0 win over Fulham at the end of 2013 didn't kick-start a run of form as they won just one point in their first five games of the new year. They only recorded four more wins in the second half of the season, beating Sunderland, Cardiff, West Brom and Swansea, and won two more points in draws, dropping them down to 16th.

Hull's squad for 2014/15 had included the likes of Harry Maguire, Andrew Robertson, Mohamed Diamé and Tom Ince. They had also signed a few players ahead of the new season as the Tigers sought to remain in the Premier League, but it didn't work out that way and they found themselves in 18th after the final day. Hull had spent most of the first half of the season in mid-table before a bad run of form knocked them down towards the danger zone. Once they sat in the bottom three, they didn't have enough to pull away completely. A brief rise to 15th was the best they could manage before a single point in the final four games saw them drop back into the relegation zone and return to the Championship.

Their first season back in the second tier had seen Tom Ince sold to Derby County for £4.75m while Robbie Brady, James Chester, Dame N'Doye and Nikica Jelavić had also left. Brady and Chester had gone to Norwich City and West Brom for £8m and £7m respectively while N'Doye and Jelavić moved to Trabzonspor and West Ham United for £2.2m and £3m. Steve Bruce did pick up Sam Clucas from Chesterfield for £1.3m and Moses Odubajo for £3.5m to replace some of the departed.

Hull did enjoy a good season, never dropping below sixth, meaning reaching at least the play-offs was inevitable. By 21 November the Tigers had lost just twice, before they fell to back-to-back defeats, although on Boxing Day, halfway through their campaign, they had taken 44 points from 23 fixtures. The second half of the season was slightly weaker than the first half: Hull were defeated six times from 28 December onwards, compared to their five defeats to that stage, but they still picked up 39 more points to finish fourth and face Derby County in the play-offs.

Playing away from home in the first leg didn't bother Hull: Abel Hernández gave them the lead with a 25-yard shot on the half-hour mark at Pride Park Stadium before an own goal from Jason Shackell doubled that lead ahead of half-time. Andrew Robertson scored late in stoppage time to secure a 3-0 win. However, the second leg was the complete opposite. Derby took an early lead with Johnny Russell netting in the seventh minute before they made it 2-0 on 36 with Robertson scoring an own goal. Goalkeeper Eldin Jakupović was on hand to deny Chris Martin a second-half equaliser as Hull held on and progressed 3-2 on aggregate.

Sheffield Wednesday faced Brighton in the other semi-final. Ross Wallace gave Wednesday the lead at Hillsborough just before half-time and Kieran Lee doubled their advantage in the 73rd minute with the first leg ending 2-0. The second encounter saw Brighton take the lead through Lewis Dunk, but less than ten minutes later Wallace's cross drifted into the goal to equalise the on the night. If the Seagulls were going to avoid a third play-off defeat in four years, they weren't going the right way about it as they barely threatened in the second half and the semi-final finished 3-1 on aggregate.

For those Hull supporters who descended on to Wembley Way, thoughts had gone back to their 2008 victory over Bristol City. They were given over 38,000 tickets this time but didn't sell out their allocation due to segregation and an ongoing boycott against their owners. The Owls had taken the majority of the 70,189 crowd, but neither set of supporters had anything to cheer after the first half with the scoreline 0-0 at the break. The only goal was in the 71st minute with a finish that was described as wonderful, brilliant and a fantastic strike; Mohamed Diamé hit an effort from outside the box and past Keiren Westwood. The victory for Hull was said to be worth at least £110m, and up to £200m over a three-year tenancy in the top flight.

However, Hull continued the trend of clubs struggling in their first season in the Premier League. After taking seven points in their opening four games and sitting sixth, the Tigers saw their form drop with just one win by the beginning of January. In that run, Hull had lost 12 times and had won just six points. They improved slightly in the new year and a win over Bournemouth was their first of six between January and late April but a haul of 21 points in the second half wasn't enough to avoid the drop.

* * *

Season 2016/17

Championship play-off final

29 May 2017

Huddersfield Town 0

Reading 0

(After extra time; Huddersfield win 4-3 on penalties)

Sky Sports and BT Sport had committed a combined £5.136bn for another three-year deal for the Premier League. Two of the UK's biggest-grouped sports channels came together in a deal that had been spurred partly by the fear of entry by beIN Sports and Eurosport. Sky had committed the lion's share, with £4.2bn, which had valued their 126 live games at £11.07m apiece.

Huddersfield Town had been far away from the riches of the Premier League in 2011/12 as they competed in League One. In the eight seasons they spent in the third tier, the Terriers had made the play-offs on four occasions: they had lost in the semi-finals against Barnsley in 2005 and Millwall in 2010 before coming closer to a place in the Championship in 2011, but lost to Peterborough United in the final. They had also made the play-offs in 2011/12, though Huddersfield had been going for automatic promotion.

That season saw Huddersfield remain undefeated in their opening 18 games. A run of ten wins and eight draws had been followed by two consecutive defeats against Charlton and Bournemouth before they lost just once more by mid-March, taking 33 points from the next 18. A win over Leyton Orient was their only victory in four games, losing the other three, before they finished the season with seven points in the final three. Huddersfield finished fourth after their mostly impressive season, facing Milton Keynes Dons in the play-off semi-final with Sheffield United and Stevenage battling it out in the other tie.

Midway through the first leg at Stadium MK, Jordan Rhodes gave the visitors the lead when he scored with a header from Lee Novak's cross. That advantage was doubled after an exchange of passes between Jack Hunt and Kallum Higginbotham had led to the former striking an effort past David Martin and putting Huddersfield 2-0 up ahead of the second leg. Three days later, Rhodes opened the scoring again, before Daniel Powell equalised from around 18 yards. Alan Smith scored a late header to give the Dons a 2-1 win on the night, but Huddersfield progressed to the final, winning 3-2 on aggregate.

The first leg between Sheffield United and Stevenage had finished goalless before the only goal in the second leg at Bramall Lane came late in the game: Chris Porter scored for the hosts with a header from a Matthew Lowton cross to help the Blades progress to Wembley.

The final on 26 May had been full of opportunities for both sides, but neither could break the deadlock. Huddersfield had enjoyed more of the chances in the early stages before Sheffield United had the better opportunities before the break. Danny Ward struck the top of the Blades' crossbar after a poor clearance in the second minute of the second half, but other efforts were sent wide of the target and the game finished 0-0.

With the score still level in extra time, Nick Montgomery cleared Peter Clarke's header off the Sheffield United goal line and penalties were required to settle it. Both sides had missed their first spot kicks: Tommy Miller's strike was easily saved by Steve Simonsen before Alex Smithies pushed Lee Williamson's effort away. Damien Johnson and Alan Lee both missed, with the latter's kick saved, but despite Neill Collins getting the Blades off the mark, Matthew Lowton and Andy Taylor missed Sheffield United's next two. Huddersfield were then faultless: Clarke, Scott Arfield, Rhodes, Gareth Roberts, Calum Woods, Hunt and Sean Morrison found the net while the Blades levelled the shoot-out with successful dispatched penalties from Chris Porter, Stephen Quinn, Maguire, Michael Doyle, Michael O'Halloran and Matthew Hill. With the score at 7-7, it came down to the goalkeepers. Smithies scored and, with Simonsen sending his effort over the bar, Huddersfield were promoted to the Championship.

In the second tier, Huddersfield had slowly improved as the seasons went by. A 19th-placed finish in 2012/13 had been followed with 17th and 16th in the two seasons that followed. They couldn't improve in 2015/16, as they ended the season in 19th. The club had spent £300,000 on Kyle Dempsey from Carlisle United during the previous season before Christopher Schindler was purchased from TSV 1860 Munich for £1.8m, while the likes of Chris Löwe and Michael Hefele had been free transfers.

The 2016/17 season was David Wagner's first full campaign in charge of the Terriers and after losing just twice in the opening 11 games, he led his team to the summit. A narrow win over Ipswich Town had been followed by a tough run of form as they won just once in the eight games that came next, taking five points in that run with draws against Birmingham and Blackburn on top of their victory. They returned to winning ways against Bristol City on 10 December, which proved to be the catalyst for another lengthy run of form for the Yorkshire side. A defeat to Sheffield Wednesday midway through January was their only defeat until 4 March as the Terriers collected 35 points in 14 games. Their end to the season saw them win five, draw once and lose seven times, securing fourth in the Championship. It was a huge improvement under German manager Wagner, but their season wasn't over as they faced Sheffield Wednesday in the play-offs.

The Terriers had failed to beat the Owls in their last seven encounters and had to settle for a goalless draw at home in the first leg, despite dominating, before travelling to Hillsborough a few days later. Steven Fletcher gave Wednesday the lead at Hillsborough but Tom Lees then gifted Huddersfield an equaliser with an own goal. The scoreline didn't change after extra time and the resulting penalty shoot-out went the way of the Terriers as they won 4-3, with goalkeeper Danny Ward the hero thanks to his two saves from Sam Hutchinson and Forestieri.

Fulham had welcomed Reading to Craven Cottage in their semi-final first leg with goals from Jordan Obita and Tom Cairney seeing the game end all square. The second leg at the Madejski saw both sides have chances, but the deciding goal came from the penalty spot. Tomáš Kalas was guilty of handling the ball and Yann Kermorgant made no mistake from 12 yards to give Reading a 2-1 aggregate win.

The final lacked chances and after 120 minutes of football there were no goals to show for it, so penalties were required. Löwe and Kermorgant scored the opening penalties before Hefele's tame effort was saved by Ali Al-Habsi. That miss allowed Danny Williams and Liam Kelly to put Reading ahead after three penalties each, despite Nahki Wells also dispatching his spot kick, but misses from Liam Moore and

Obita allowed Aaron Mooy and Schindler to secure victory for Huddersfield.

The Terriers went on to spend two seasons in the Premier League. In 2017/18 they won their opening two games, putting them top of the table for two weeks, before they won a further two games while drawing six and losing nine by the end of the year. The second half of the season saw the Terriers win just three more and take 13 points in 17 games, but despite that dip they survived relegation and finished 16th.

The following season was far more difficult, with Huddersfield sitting in the relegation zone for all but five weeks. Two of Huddersfield's three total wins had come in November before their third and final one arrived in February against Wolverhampton Wanderers. The Terriers had taken ten points in the first half of the season and only another six to the end of the season saw them relegated.

* * *

Season 2017/18

Championship play-off final

26 May 2018

Aston Villa 0

Fulham 1 (Cairney 23)

Fulham's first two seasons back in the Championship following their relegation at the end of the 2013/14 season had seen them finish 17th and 20th before they made a huge improvement in 2016/17. An unbeaten start to the season with three wins and two draws was followed by just one win in the next nine games. The Cottagers then had mixed form, with it being on the better side for the most part: six wins, four draws and two losses had taken them through to the new year before they lost three of their first six games in 2017. By February, Fulham had discovered some consistency and despite three losses to Birmingham, Wolves and Derby County, they snuck into the play-offs after winning 12 and drawing four, facing Reading in the play-off semi-final.

Jordan Obita gave Reading the lead in the 53rd minute at Craven Cottage before Tom Cairney equalised just under ten minutes later, with the game ending level. The sides met at the Madejski Stadium three days later and the only goal of the second leg was scored from the penalty spot by Reading's Yann Kermorgant four minutes into the second half. That defeat left Fulham competing in the Championship for another year.

Three successive draws to begin 2017/18 were followed by mixed form that kept Fulham mid-table for most of the season. Seven wins, five more draws and seven defeats put them 12th before they slowly rose towards the play-offs after a lengthy good run from 23

December. It had begun with a 2-1 win over Barnsley and spanned 23 games with Fulham winning 59 points before a final-day defeat against Birmingham at St Andrew's. Their incredible form had seen them force their way to third in the table, facing sixth-placed Derby County in the play-offs.

Fulham dominated the first leg but had found themselves 1-0 down after Cameron Jerome struck the only goal for Derby. Fulham were again well on top in the second leg and, with two second-half goals from Ryan Sessegnon and Denis Odoi, the west Londoners won 2-1 on aggregate and progressed to the final.

In the other semi-final, Aston Villa faced Middlesbrough with the first leg at the Riverside Stadium. It was won by a single goal, Mile Jedinak scoring a first-half header in a game with few chances. The return leg then ended goalless meaning Villa's victory on Teesside had been enough to send them through to the final, though Boro had almost forced extra time, but Stewart Downing's direct free kick struck the crossbar in the last minute.

The final was described in the build-up as a classic clash of styles, pitching an experienced Villa against a youthful Fulham, with victory said to be worth up to £160m over three years in the Premier League. It was won by the youth talent of Fulham as a 23rd-minute strike from Tom Cairney was the difference.

Fulham's return to the Premier League saw them spend big in pursuit of survival. They signed Jean Michaël Seri from Nice for £18m, striker Aleksandar Mitrović for £22m from Newcastle, Alfie Mawson for £15m from Swansea and Joe Bryan for £6m from Bristol City.

The 2018/19 season started with two consecutive losses against Crystal Palace and

Tottenham, putting them 19th in the table, before they briefly moved away from the relegation zone with a run of five points in four games. Fulham spent six weeks out of the bottom three before they bounced between the bottom three spots as the season went on. They won just three times in the first half and four times in the second half, and their haul of 26 points left them ten points off safety.

* * *

Season 2018/19

Championship play-off final

27 May 2019

Aston Villa 2 (El Ghazi 44; McGinn 59)

Derby County 1 (Marriott 81)

Aston Villa's disappointment at missing out on promotion to the Premier League in 2018 was quickly forgotten as they returned to the play-off final the following season, claiming their spot in the top flight with victory over Derby County.

The campaign had seen the Villans win their first two before drawing the next three and sitting pretty in the play-off positions. Their form dropped as they won two of the ten games that followed, taking a total of nine points in that time. Villa returned to winning ways on 2 November against Bolton Wanderers before they won five, drew five and lost once by January. Another dip saw them win six points in seven matches before they went 12 unbeaten, taking 32 points. A loss on the final day against Norwich City didn't matter as Villa finished fifth.

They were joined in the play-offs by Leeds United, West Bromwich Albion and Derby County with the order of finishes creating an all-West Midlands derby while Leeds were pitted against the Rams.

In their first leg at Villa Park, the hosts found themselves a goal down after Dwight Gayle scored for the Baggies before two goals in three minutes for Aston Villa saw them win 2-1: Conor Hourihane struck the first from 25 yards to draw them level before Tammy Abraham scored a penalty. The return leg saw West Brom take the lead once again, Craig Dawson scoring in the 29th minute to level the semi-final on aggregate. Villa dominated the match, but failed to score a winner before a goalless period of extra time sent the game to penalties. Two saves from Villa goalkeeper Jed Steer allowed Abraham to score the winning spot kick and send Aston Villa to their second consecutive final.

Derby had lost their first leg at Pride Park against Leeds after a second-half Kemar Roofe goal, then came a second leg described as a wild night. Stuart Dallas had doubled Leeds' aggregate advantage midway through the first half before goals from Jack Marriott, Mason Mount and Harry Wilson put Derby 3-2 up on the night.

Dallas then netted his second goal midway through the second half but Marriott ensured the Rams' participation in the final with a late strike, securing a 4-3 aggregate win for Frank Lampard's men, who became the first team in the history of the second-tier play-offs to lose at home in the first leg but then come back to reach the final.

Over 85,000 supporters arrived at Wembley to see Villa take the lead late in the first half through Anwar El Ghazi, after the winger dived between two defenders and scored with his shoulder. They were 2-0 up on the hour when John McGinn beat goalkeeper Kelle Roos to a looping ball after El Ghazi's shot took a deflection, with the midfielder heading it home. Derby fans had something to cheer in the 81st minute as substitute Marriott reduced the deficit, but it wasn't enough for a comeback as they lost 2-1.

Villa's return to the Premier League saw them finish 17th. They spent heavy in the summer in the transfer market as they sought to remain in the top flight with the signings of Wesley (£22m), Kortney Hause (£3m), Matt Targett (£11.5m), Tyrone Mings (£20m), Ezri Konsa (£12m), Björn Engels (£9m), Trézéguet (£8.75m), Douglas Luiz (£15m), Tom Heaton (£8m) and Marvelous Nakamba (£10.2m). The £120m spent by Villa barely kept them in the Premier League, but a haul of 35 points in their 38 games saw them finish a point above Bournemouth. Since then, Villa have remained in the top flight, going on to play Champions League football in 2024/25.

* * *

Season 2019/20

4 August 2020

Brentford 1 (Dalsgaard 120+4)

Fulham 2 (Bryan 105, 117)

(After extra time)

The television deal agreed ahead of the 2019/20 season had included packages sold to Sky Sports, BT Sport and Amazon. The combination of deals awarded to the three broadcasters had been worth £4.8bn, giving Premier League clubs a bigger prize at the end of the season.

Fulham had their eyes on a return to the Premier League after a disappointing 2018/19 campaign, which saw them relegated back to the Championship. A loss to Barnsley on the opening day of 2019/20 had left them in the relegation zone before they rose up the table. After they beat Queens Park Rangers in

November, the Cottagers found themselves in the play-off places, where they remained until the end of the season. For Fulham, it hadn't been a question of whether they would make the play-offs, but which position they would occupy. They had bounced between all the play-off positions before they settled in fourth and had seen out the campaign with 17 points in their final seven games.

Fulham faced Cardiff City in the semi-final and were on the road for the first leg. They were without their top scorer, Aleksandar Mitrović, but they didn't need him as Josh Onomah fired them ahead four minutes into the second half. They dominated the remainder of the match and doubled their advantage in injury time when Neeskens Kebano scored directly from a free kick. The second leg was three days later with Curtis Nelson heading Cardiff ahead after eight minutes, but that lead lasted for just 24 seconds as Kebano restored Fulham's two-goal aggregate advantage, converting a cross from Bobby De Cordova-Reid from 12 yards. Two minutes into the second half, Lee Tomlin scored Cardiff's second with a volley, but despite losing the second leg 2-1, it was Fulham who progressed to the final.

The other London side, Brentford, travelled to Wales like their capital counterparts and after a goalless first half between them and Swansea City, a half-volley from André Ayew gave the hosts a 1-0 lead with less than ten minutes remaining. The second leg came three days later and was the last match at Griffin Park before the Bees moved to their new home. Ollie Watkins levelled the tie on aggregate after 11 minutes before Emiliano Marcondes scored with a header to put Brentford ahead. Bryan Mbeumo scored with a volley from a Rico Henry cross one minute into the second half and Rhian Brewster scored for Swansea with 12 minutes remaining, but the home win for Brentford was enough for them to progress to the final with a 3-2 aggregate result.

Due to the Covid-19 pandemic, the final didn't take place until 4 August because of the delay to the conclusion of the regular season, which was held up between March and June, and it was played behind closed doors. The 90 minutes were not eventful and finished goalless before it kicked into life in extra time. The deadlock was broken in the 105th minute when Joe Bryan struck a 40-yard free kick over David Raya, who was off his goal line. Fulham then all but confirmed their spot in the Premier League after a goal in the 117th minute made it 2-0, as a good passage of play between Bryan and Mitrović allowed the former to net his second of the game. Henrik Dalsgaard scored for Brentford from a Christian Nørgaard header with less than a minute to play, but it was nothing more than a consolation.

Scott Parker led Fulham in their return to the Premier League, but it didn't go as they had hoped and they were relegated again at the end of the 2020/21 season. The highest they sat in the table was 17th following wins against West Brom and Leicester in November, but after spending 35 weeks in the relegation zone, Fulham's card was already marked.

The 2020s

Season 2020/21

29 May 2021

Brentford 2 (Toney 10 pen; Marcondes 20)

Swansea City 0

THE TARGET for Brentford for the 2020/21 season was simple: secure promotion to the Premier League. It was the Bees' first year at their new home, the Brentford Community Stadium, and they had purchased striker Ivan Toney from Peterborough United for £5m.

After the disappointment of the previous campaign, it was paramount that Brentford got off to the best possible start. Instead, they took ten points in seven games before a draw at home to Norwich City kick-started an impressive unbeaten run: between late October and February, the Bees won 13 of their 21 games, drawing the other eight. It came to an end on 14 February with a loss to Barnsley followed by another two defeats, against QPR and Coventry City, before Brentford finished the season with just one reverse in 15 games, winning eight and drawing six. Their record propelled them to third place, qualifying them for the play-offs alongside Swansea City, Barnsley and Bournemouth.

Brentford faced Bournemouth in the semi-final and after a goalless first half at Dean Court, Arnaut Danjuma scored on the counterattack in the 55th minute from a through ball from David Brooks. It was the only goal of the game, and the second leg was played five days later. Danjuma again scored the opening goal to increase Bournemouth's aggregate score before Brentford were awarded a penalty 11 minutes later, Toney dispatching the spot kick to pull a goal back. Just after half-time, Vitaly Janelt scored for Brentford to make it 2-1 on the day and, with nine minutes remaining, Marcus Forss scored for the hosts to make it 3-1, sending the Bees through to the final with a 3-2 aggregate win.

André Ayew had given the Swans the lead in their semi-final first leg at Oakwell in the 39th minute with a curling left-footed shot past Bradley Collins in the Barnsley goal. Carlton Morris came closest for the Tykes when he rattled the Swansea crossbar in injury time, but it finished 1-0. The second leg was played five days later, Matt Grimes extending the home side's aggregate lead six minutes before half-time with a curling strike before

Cauley Woodrow scored for Barnsley in the 71st minute, striking a ball from the edge of the Swansea penalty area. The 2-1 win on aggregate had sealed the Welsh club's place at Wembley.

The final at the end of May was exactly where Brentford wanted to spend their Saturday afternoon, and their hopes of finally reaching the Premier League moved a step closer to reality when they were awarded a penalty in the tenth minute. Bryan Mbeumo was fouled by goalkeeper Freddie Woodman with Toney stepping up to give Brentford the lead. The domination from the London side continued and they doubled their advantage ten minutes later: Brentford went on the counterattack, Mbeumo passed to Mads Roerslev, whose cross was finished by Emiliano Marcondes. There were no further goals, and it was tenth time lucky for the Bees, who had fallen short in their nine previous play-off attempts beginning with the 1990/91 Third Division semi-final.

Brentford finished 13th in their first season in the Premier League before coming ninth and 16th in the next two years. At the time of writing they sat comfortably in mid-table as the 2024/25 season approached its close.

* * *

Season 2021/22

29 May 2022

Huddersfield Town 0

Nottingham Forest 1 (Colwill 43 og)

One point in seven games at the start of the 2021/22 season cost Chris Hughton his job at Nottingham Forest, with Steve Cooper taking over from 21 September. The new manager made a decent start to his tenure, losing just once in a run of 16 games that saw his side win 33 points. Back-to-back defeats against Middlesbrough and Huddersfield Town in December were followed by a run of 14 wins, four draws and three losses, seeing the Reds finish miraculously fourth.

They ended up two points below third-placed Huddersfield Town, meaning they faced Sheffield United in the semi-finals instead of Luton Town, with the first leg taking place at Bramall Lane on 14 May. The visitors took an early lead when Jack Colback scored a rebound from a Wes Foderingham save. Brennan Johnson made it 2-0 with less than 20 minutes remaining after taking advantage of an error from John Egan. One minute into injury time, Sander Berge scored from a Morgan Gibbs-White corner to halve the deficit, but Forest took a 2-1 lead into the second leg, which took place three days later at the City Ground. Forest saw their aggregate lead extended when Johnson scored, before goals from Gibbs-White and John Fleck in the second half levelled it up and forced extra time. The additional 30 minutes didn't change the scoreline and it went to penalties. Home goalkeeper Brice Samba kept out three of the visitors' spot kicks and Nottingham Forest won the shoot-out 3-2.

Luton went a goal down to Huddersfield despite being at home in their first leg. Danel Sinani opened the scoring in the 12th minute after Harry Toffolo passed the ball forward, before the Hatters equalised through Sonny Bradley from a Kal Naismith free kick. Though the Terriers controlled the second half, the first leg finished level. The second leg three days later saw just one goal, with Jordan Rhodes scoring from close range eight minutes from full time to give Huddersfield a 1-0 victory and 2-1 win on aggregate.

If anyone had expected an open, free-flowing contest from the final, they would have been disappointed. While the teams taking part had finished in the top two play-off spots, it was still a nervy affair. The only goal of the contest came just before half-time when Levi Colwill scored an own goal: James Garner crossed the ball into the Huddersfield penalty area towards Ryan Yates but an unfortunate ricochet off the Chelsea loanee gifted the Reds a place in the Premier League.

Their return to the top flight saw them finish 16th, two points ahead of the bottom three, and a year later they came 17th, six points above the drop zone. But a strong first two thirds of 2024/25 had them not worried about relegation at all and instead eyeing a remarkable qualification for the Champions League, sitting comfortably in the top three by the spring.

* * *

Season 2022/23

27 May 2023

Coventry City 1 (Hamer 66)

Luton Town 1 (Clark 23)

(After extra time; Luton win 6-5 on penalties)

Under the management of Nathan Jones, Luton Town sat ninth in the Championship on 8 November 2022. The Hatters had missed out on promotion the previous season, losing 2-1 to Huddersfield Town on aggregate in the play-off semi-final, and had a decent start to 2022/23: two points in the opening four games had been followed by a run of one defeat in 11 games as they rose to fourth. They did drop down to ninth after winning just five points in as many games, which also cost Jones his job.

Rob Edwards, who had managed Luton's rivals Watford before taking the job at Kenilworth

Road, had got off to the perfect start after beating both QPR and Norwich City, taking the club back into the play-off spots before a dip in form had seen them fall to ninth once more. A defeat to Watford was followed by just one win in seven games before they lost just twice more. A goalless draw against Millwall almost halfway through a 14-game unbeaten run pushed them as high as third, where they finished the season.

The play-offs began on 13 May with Luton facing Sunderland. The first leg at the Stadium of Light saw Luton take the lead in the 11th minute after the hosts had failed to clear a corner and Elijah Adebayo scored from a rebound shot after Alfie Doughty's close-range strike was saved by Anthony Patterson. The game was level just before half-time when Amad Diallo curled the ball into the top corner beyond Luton goalkeeper Ethan Horvath. Sunderland built on their momentum and took the lead in the 63rd minute: Trai Hume scored with a header from a Jack Clarke cross and the game finished 2-1. The second leg took place three days later with Luton scoring in the tenth minute: Tom Lockyer won the ball from a corner and the ball fell to Gabriel Osho who reacted quickest to score. They added a second in the 43rd minute when an in-swinging cross from Doughty was met by Lockyer to make it 2-0. It finished that way, sending the Hatters into the final with a 3-2 win on aggregate.

Coventry City met Middlesbrough in the other semi-final, but their goalless first leg was described as poor and tense as they managed two shots on target between them, with both coming from Middlesbrough. The second leg wasn't much better; the only goal arrived in the 57th minute after Middlesbrough lost possession on the halfway line. Coventry's Viktor Gyökeres played the ball into space beyond Zack Steffan before Gustavo

Hamer hit his shot into the roof of the net. Middlesbrough did have the ball in the back of the net with two minutes to go, but it was ruled out for offside, and Coventry progressed with a narrow aggregate win.

Both finalists had won promotion from League Two in 2017/18: the Hatters finished second and secured automatic promotion while the Sky Blues came through the play-offs, beating Exeter City 3-1, so both sides meeting at Wembley for a place in the Premier League five years later showed the romance of the game. There had been concern that Luton would struggle on the vast space of the Wembley pitch, but they had found themselves ahead after Adebayo carved out an opening for Jordan Clark, who smashed a stunning screamer just inside the post after 23 minutes. A little over 20 minutes into the second half, Coventry found themselves level. Gyökeres had held up the ball and turned it into the path of Hamer, who bent it into the bottom corner. It was still all square after 90 minutes. Then there were no further goals in extra time; Luton did have two goals disallowed across the course of the 120 minutes.

In a shoot-out to decide the victor, both sides converted their five penalties: Matt Godden, Gyökeres, Ben Sheaf, Josh Eccles and Liam Kelly were on target for Coventry while Morris, Joe Taylor, Marvelous Nakamba, Clark and Luke Berry did the same for the Hatters. It came down to sudden death and Dan Potts made no mistake before Fankaty Dabo hit his effort high and wide to send Luton into the Premier League for the first time, completing their remarkable turnaround – having been relegated from the old First Division in 1991/92, the season before the Premier League began, they fell all the way into non-league football before reaching the top tier again.

However, Luton found life in the Premier League tough in 2023/24. Four straight losses against Brighton, Chelsea, West Ham United and Fulham left them bottom of the table before they picked up their first point in a 1-1 draw with Wolves. That was followed by their first win, beating Everton, with the Hatters taking five points in the next six games. From 23 December, Luton won four, drew five and lost 13, putting them 18th, and despite sitting in the relegation zone for most of the season, their fall back to the Championship wasn't confirmed until the final day after a 4-2 defeat to Fulham and with other results from across the league.

* * *

To get an insight into Luton Town's promotion to the Premier League, I spoke to Luton season ticket holder Robson O'Reardon.

Luton Town were playing in League One as recently as 2018/19. Did you ever think they would reach the Premier League?

RO'R: I always believed we had the potential to compete in the Premier League someday, but I never anticipated it would happen so quickly. While the financial benefits of promotion to the Premier League are fantastic, I think it all happened too soon for the club, and we just weren't ready for the step up.

After winning League One, the club kept slowly improving as each season went by. How good was the rise from their League One triumph?

RO'R: It was fantastic! I was surprised by how quickly we improved after our promotion from League One. Except for one challenging season when Nathan Jones stepped in to rescue us from relegation, our growth as a team in such a brief time was truly remarkable.

Nathan Jones was manager from May 2020, Luton finishing 19th that season. He went on to reach finishes of 12th and sixth before leaving in November 2022. Had he taken the club as far as he could?

RO'R: The fanbase is divided when it comes to Nathan Jones. While some hold resentment towards him for leaving the club twice [Jones had earlier been in charge of Luton from January 2016 to January 2019], others expressed a desire for his return after Edwards left the club. In my opinion, he did an excellent job for us and deserves recognition for putting together most of the squad that led Luton to the Premier League.

Rob Edwards took over, having been let go from Watford. Did you expect him to have such a great impact at the club?

RO'R: It's difficult to determine. When Edwards came to Luton, I felt a mix of excitement and apprehension, especially given his background as a former Watford manager. Initially, he made a significant impact, truly grasping what it meant to be a Hatter and embracing everything the club represented. His legacy will be cherished, but I believe the choice to part ways with him was made far too late, and now we find ourselves facing the threat of relegation [from the Championship in 2024/25; Edwards left Kenilworth Road in January 2025].

Having been 18th in September, the club finished third in 2022/23. What were your expectations for the play-offs?

RO'R: We've participated in numerous play-offs in recent years so, honestly, I had no expectations. Approaching these types of games with that mindset is often the best strategy. Of course, I would have been disappointed if we had lost, but I had a strong belief that we had what it took to succeed.

A tough semi-final first leg at Sunderland resulted in a defeat. How confident were you that you'd turn it around at home?

RO'R: To be completely honest, I didn't feel confident at all! While it may sound pessimistic, Sunderland were a strong team and played exceptionally well against us. The atmosphere in the second leg had to be electric and it was.

You faced Coventry in the final and it proved to be a tight game. Did you think the nerves got the better of both sides?

RO'R: I believe that scoring early on, even though it was ruled out for offside, helped ease our nerves a bit. When Tom Lockyer went down early in the match, it made everyone anxious and concerned for his wellbeing. From that point forward, the players seemed to shed their nerves.

* * *

Season 2023/24

26 May 2024

Leeds United 0

Southampton 1 (Armstrong 24)

The 2023/24 Championship play-off final had given both Leeds and Southampton the opportunity to immediately return to the Premier League after they had been relegated at the end of the 2022/23 season.

The Saints had an almost perfect start to life in the Championship as they won three and drew one of their opening four games before they then suffered four consecutive defeats. A win over Leeds then got them back on track and they went 23 games unbeaten between the end of September and mid-February. Another loss, this time to Bristol City, was followed by a win over West Brom before two defeats at St

Mary's Stadium against Hull City and Millwall. In March, they took seven points from three games before they followed that up with a run of four wins, one draw and four losses in the final nine matches.

The South Coast side finished fourth, three points behind Leeds but ahead of West Brom and Norwich City, with the Saints facing the Baggies in the semi-final, travelling to The Hawthorns for the first leg. That game finished goalless before the sides met at St Mary's on 17 May. Southampton opened the scoring in the second half as Will Smallbone struck the ball beyond Alex Palmer, before Adam Armstrong doubled the lead in the 78th minute. Less than ten minutes later, Southampton were awarded a penalty for a foul on Ryan Manning with Armstrong converting it for his second of the night, before Cédric Kipré scored a header in injury time to give West Brom a consolation.

Leeds' first leg with Norwich at Carrow Road had also ended goalless. Ilia Gruev deceived Canaries goalkeeper Angus Gunn to make it 1-0 in the seventh minute of the return at Elland Road, before Joël Piroe doubled their lead in the 20th minute with a header from a Wilfried Gnonto cross. Georginio Rutter further extended their advantage in the 40th minute and Crysencio Summerville made it 4-0 on 68. The rampant win at home had sealed a 4-0 aggregate victory, sending Leeds to Wembley.

The final was on 26 May and, although seven goals had been scored between the sides in their respective semi-finals, it was far from a goal-fest. Adam Armstrong gave Southampton the lead in the 24th minute when Flynn Downes played a pass into Smallbone, who slotted the ball through to Armstrong with the forward firing the shot into the bottom corner. With it being the only goal of the game, the Saints held on to secure an immediate return to the Premier League.

At the time of writing, Southampton were adrift at the bottom of the table, taking 24 games to reach nine points. While breaking Derby County's unwanted Premier League record low of 11 points was looking unlikely, they appeared to be running out of time to avoid relegation.